Ecommerce Product Management

BOOK OF GROWTH

Darius Vasefi

Build your SYSTEM of Growth for ecommerce.

ISBN: 9798873361946

Version 1.0

Publisher: BooDaa Publishing, San Clemente, CA

Boodaa Publishing educational books are available at special quantity discounts to use as premiums and sales promotions for use in corporate training programs. To discuss a volume purchase, speaking engagements or corporate training please email pub@infiniventures.com.

CONTENTS

Dedicated to **Navideh** and **Booboo**, my forever friends without whose love, support and wisdom I would never be able to accomplish this endeavor.

Intro

Welcome to the life of a product manager.

An educator, explorer and a pragmatic business person with an eye on the data, customer experience, feedback, performance and another eye on growth and sometimes, finances.

Indeed a critical role in today's digital organizations.

Before the role of Product Manager had become prevalent and better known I, similar to many other product professionals, came to this new role and function accidentally.

Already doing the work for over a decade, I only learned about the formal role of a "product manager", when a recruiter contacted me.

Back then we were just founders and product builders, but the product manager took that role and molded it to work inside corporations, specially the largest digital corporations such as Amazon, Apple, Microsoft, Google, Facebook, Uber and Netflix as well as every new technology startup.

Understanding the details of the role it started to make sense that this was a key part of what I had been doing but under a different title. I suspect many other product builders and founders might find this familiar when they think about their work.

Nowadays the product manager role is better understood in digital organizations and an industry has formed thanks to the many amazing and smart leaders having paved the road for the rest of us.

As a product manager, you may have a similar path to mine or completely different. Or you might be looking into growing into a product role. Either way being a product manager can be not only a fulfilling personal growth journey but also a rewarding career.

You may also have accepted new responsibilities which include product organizations and are looking to become more informed to lead product organizations.

In all these cases a more systematic way of organizing, experimenting and measuring our work will reduce ambiguity, subjectivity and potential for unproductive internal politics.

While the foundations and best practices of the product management profession are taking shape there are still differences in how product managers function are thought of and utilized in different companies.

This evolution of the role is not just for the practitioners but also the executive leadership of companies who are responsible for planning, hiring and leading the teams that build and grow their products, including product managers.

Being a relatively new role, many executive leaders in large companies do not yet understand the true role of product managers, and unfortunately think of and utilize them more as project managers.

This discrepancy is most obvious when you see people doing the work of project and program managers and having the title of product managers.

I personally advocate for all company executive leaders to educate themselves on what the role of a product manager is and not delegate this only to the Chief Product Officer and VPs of Product. Every leader in the new digital organization should be well versed in what is a product manager and how it differs from other roles including project and program management, both important functions.

Author's notes

Ecommerce, as part of the overall retail industry, is here to stay. There have, and will be up- and down-cycles but the overall trend is to improve and grow.

And as a highly specialized industry ecommerce is evolving by leaps and bounds, on multiple fronts. From consumer trends and behavior, product categories, business models, User Experience (UX) and various front-end technologies to server side back-end, security, privacy and more there are truly hundreds of specific and unique techniques, processes and gotchas awaiting the professionals building, running and growing ecommerce companies.

At the same time the skills and teams involved in managing all these different pieces of the puzzle are also highly specialized and evolving to meet the demands of consumers and business.

One of these roles is the Product Manager often referred to as the product CEO, the glue, the facilitator and the owner - often a combination of all these. The expectations and demands are typically high, and often this is where the buck stops, at least on specific products or features.

There are hundreds of books, blogs, podcasts and channels focused on ecommerce but not many which specifically cater to the product management side.

My goal in writing this book is to contribute to the amazing work in building the future of commerce and retail by product managers as well as introduce and inform other interested, enthusiasts and involved professionals in the space.

Of course it is not possible to cover all the different parts of ecommerce in one book so this will be a series of books on the topic. The first book in the series, this book is focused on Growth since growth is on the top of the list of business goals and expectations from product managers. In addition there will be an accompanying tool to dive deeper into every topic and stay current.

This is just the nature of the business we're in - change is constant on all fronts and for any publication to be relevant it must keep up with the change and this is my attempt at doing so.

My goal is that this book and the accompanying tools will help product managers enhance their impact on products and organizations they create or are involved in, and in more measurable and quantifiable ways over time.

My background

As a Mechanical Engineer and technology explorer I've always been intrigued with the way software can help our lives better.

For over 30 years I have started, ran and sold companies in software services, applications in ecommerce, retail technology, SaaS (Software as a Service), business productivity and in general solving problems I find interesting and worthy to solve.

My journey has taken me inside the world's largest enterprises such as Walmart, Amazon, Verizon, Oracle and many more as well as startups of one, on top of being an adjunct professor in the University of California system for many years.

I think of myself as a student and builder first, then a teacher, mentor and guide.

As a builder and innovator, the function of Product Manager has been specially fitting for me when it comes to operations and company building so I have invested the last decade of my work specifically in understanding, learning, practicing and contributing to the practice.

I have built teams of hundreds of technology and product professionals and thousands of retail members, and am humbled and honored daily by the team members who choose to join our products and most of all look forward to learning from every single team member..

This book is a part of my ongoing work on that front. I hope you find value in it for your career and life!

Who is this book for

This book is first and foremost for product managers in the ecommerce and retail space, and more specifically for those responsible and focused on growth.

Around the product manager there is a vast team and network of direct and indirect roles interfacing and collaborating with the role. From designers for the product experience and User Interface to analytics, marketing, management, and the technical team.

For people who want to move into the role of product management, this book will give you practical, from the trenches knowledge to play the role even before you get the title, and raise the bar after you take on the responsibility.

And for the business leaders who are tasked with hiring and leading product teams this book will help you form a larger and more informed view of what ecommerce product managers and growth could, and likely should do. The bar can be raised for the team and the organization.

*Build your **system** for growth, and success!*

Setting expectations

Let's start by setting some expectations and ground rules:

- **All our work is Work-in-Progress (WIP):** Tools, techniques, experiences and options in ecommerce and growth are constantly evolving and expanding. What I've included in this book IS NOT a fully comprehensive list of all the available tools and options. In order to help with keeping current with an ever-changing and evolving I have created a companion site and tools, see Closing for information.
- **PdM vs. PM:** in professional product circles you'll see references to product managers as PMs, whereas historically this acronym was used for project managers, or program managers. What we are seeing happen in today's modern product organizations is the slow transition from project to product, and from waterfall to agile. In agile the role of project manager is usually performed by Scrum Masters (SM) and we don't see many project manager roles any more. This is just a small sampling and reference to technology companies where project management is prevalent in many other industries, where product managers are not as necessary for example construction and large scale waterfall projects.
  - Respectively, in this book I will use PM to refer to the Product Manager role.
- **Strong opinions:** you might (will) read some strong opinions in this book. These are my opinions based on my experience and what I have learned and guide me in my work.
- **AI tool assistance:** as this is not a book of fiction and we live in the 21st century, I have in preparation for writing this book utilized the help of multiple people and tools including writing and publishing consultants, research assistants, design and business experts, and yes even AI tools. But I can attest that the entire idea, organization, final written manuscript and management of the book are original and from me.

- **Distinguishing between product and marketing in Growth:** growth has many paths and functions including marketing and product management. My focus in this book is the role of product managers in growth, not marketing. There are extensive resources available on marketing customer acquisition and marketers are a key partner to product managers.

However, the types of growth activities each of these roles can enable and run are different and it's best to have focus instead of mixing up all growth into one role.

An added point here is that even though I am separating marketing from product, I in no way mean that product managers should not understand marketing. In fact the best product managers, especially for growth understand the principles of marketing well and stay current on what their marketing counterparts do.

Book organization

The information in this book is organized into Horizontal and Vertical areas.

Horizontal skills and practices

Horizontal information or skills are those all product managers need to understand and practice. Of course there is a focus on Growth here but as I have and will mention several times growth should be a part of every product manager's role, even if your specific title is not a growth product manager.

Horizontal information does not apply to a specific vertical, for example ecommerce, or health tech, fintech or Saas. This information goes across industry and product verticals.

Horizontal skills are typically transferable across different product categories, unless the role is highly technical in which case those could be considered a vertical skillset.

Vertical skills and tools

Vertical information is specifically about ecommerce and retail. This is information that a SaaS PM does not necessarily need to know to grow her products. Vertical information and expertise is not easily transferable to other product categories.

Vertical expertise is the next level of specialization for product managers and it's important for hiring managers to assess and bring onboard product managers with vertical experience to their product lines. If you hire someone with years of SaaS product experience into an ecommerce company that person will NOT be fully productive out of the gate and will require months or likely years of additional experience to become a fully contributing part of your team.

And my personal opinion is that there are no jacks of all trades when it comes to vertical specializations. A bit off topic here butMany people talk about full-stack

Part One can be thought of as horizontal skills. No matter what tools or methodologies we're focusing on, we'll always require horizontal skills and practices to get the job done.

In Part Two, we will look at the "vertical" aspects of ecommerce growth.

Part One

Setting the foundation for successful ecommerce product management.

Product management: A background

Product manager, on one hand, is a hybrid of product marketing and product development and on the other hand, it's product strategy, integration, application and growth.

In modern organizations, the role of the Chief Product Officer (CPO) extends to the senior leadership levels, carrying significant responsibility and influence. An increasing number of startup founders and CEOs have a background in product management.

As a relatively new profession, there are not yet many standardized expectations and structures in place. The role tends to adapt and mold itself to fit the organization.

Product managers have two main components to their work:

- Core product management skills
- Industry and product specific skills

There are many great resources on the core product skills, some of which I touch on in Part One.

Industry-specific skills for product managers complete the package and require ongoing education and experience to master and stay relevant.For example industries such as medical software or hardware, financial or fintech, ecommerce, and omni-channel retail each have their unique nuances and require specific skill sets that product managers in these fields must possess.

In addition, there is expectation and responsibility to businesses for improving performance and the key performance indicators (KPIs), which is why sometimes product managers are called product CEOs.

Types of ecommerce

As an industry, ecommerce encompasses any application or service that enables customers to view a variety of product options, purchase the products online, and obtain the products they have purchased.

The process of managing products for an ecommerce business is referred to as ecommerce product management. It entails the design, development, and implementation of strategies to maximize the sales and profitability of online-sold products.

There are several business models utilizing ecommerce, including:

- Ecommerce retailer
- Ecommerce operation of a retailer, aka omni-channel commerce
- Ecommerce marketplaces
- Direct-to-consumer (D2C)
- Ecommerce and shopping apps
- P2P (peer-to-peer)
- Other websites and apps process online transactions.

Ecommerce product management requires an in-depth understanding of the target market and consumer behavior, as well as the ability to use data and analytics to inform decision-making.

It also requires collaborating with marketing, design, and technology teams to present items in the best light.

Overall, ecommerce product management is vital to the success of an ecommerce business because it ensures that the right products are available to the right consumers at the right time and price.

Ecommerce is eating (a part) of retail!

As the famous entrepreneur and investor Marc Andreesen said "software is eating the world."

Over the past 30 years, we have observed a significant rise in ecommerce, which currently accounts for approximately 20% of the retail industry as of 2023.

But we're not done with the change in our shopping habits and methods.

It appears that the rate of change is indeed accelerating, and innovation is becoming unstoppable. In the past 30 years, we have witnessed significant transformative changes. However, it is highly probable that we are merely at the dawn of a new era of transformation in the realm of commerce and online shopping. This new era is characterized by the emergence of various types of artificial intelligence, such as Generative AI, Blockchain, Crypto currencies, Virtual reality (VR), and the Metaverse.

What is Growth

Growth in an ecommerce business involves the enhancement of Key Performance Indicators (KPIs). These metrics have a significant impact on customers, the business itself, and other stakeholders. By improving these indicators, the organization can operate more efficiently and generate higher profits.

We have a few levers to pull to grow ecommerce and retail businesses:

- Find more customers, including all activities for the Acquisition function.
- Help customers become clients (a client is a customer you have made a longer term relationship with). This is the Engagement piece involving activities to keep existing customers happy so they continue buying from the company.
- Improve unit economics, which is identifying and implementing cost efficiencies and margin expansion where possible in the entire cycle of business without negatively impacting customer experience.
- Reduce churn, which is your customers not purchasing from you any more. This is referred to as Retention to detect when a customer is nearing drop off and taking action in various forms to help them stay a client.
- The final, and most important, piece is focusing on the lifetime value (LTV) of customers also referred to as CLV or CLTV. Lifetime value, in my experience, is the most important gauge of the potential of a business. As a business if your LTV potential is low you will have a much harder time growing than if you have potential for a larger LTV. All your other activities roll up to increasing the customer lifetime value.

Most businesses have the potential to create large LTVs, either directly or indirectly, but not all businesses capitalize on this potential!

Expanding LTV (customer Lifetime Value) requires creativity and thinking outside the box. While acquisition and retention are also important, engagement is arguably the most crucial factor as it has the greatest impact on LTV.

One challenge that many high-flying ecommerce businesses faced in the 2010s was an excessive focus on customer acquisition. These businesses were successful in acquiring new customers, even though they did so at a loss. However, they were unable to generate a high lifetime value (LTV) or did not effectively capitalize on this potential.

If you only sell one product, such as mattresses, and have a low frequency of customer acquisition, your customer acquisition costs (CAC) will be very high and the lifetime value (LTV) of each customer will be limited.

Growth is a continuous cycle and does not end. And it's the fuel driving the engine of business pushing or pulling all the other functions to keep up.

The most effective growth systems leverage a combination of human expertise and automated tools to empower humans to utilize their unique abilities in instinct, judgment, and original thinking.

Tools are required for effective planning, tracking, measuring, reporting, and insights, all the way up to automated decision making for the operation's optimum performance.

Other factors impacting growth are technological advancements, changes in consumer behavior, and shifts in the overall economy.

Growth for ecommerce businesses can be measured in various ways, such as by the number of online shoppers, the total volume of online sales, or the percentage of total retail sales that occur online. Regardless of the specific metric used, the trend is clear: e-commerce is growing at a rapid pace and is likely to continue to do so in the coming years.

Some of the key drivers of e-commerce growth include the increasing use of mobile devices for online shopping, the rise of social media as a marketing tool, and the growing popularity of online marketplaces such as Amazon and eBay.

Additionally, the COVID-19 pandemic has accelerated the shift to online shopping, as many consumers were forced to stay home and avoid in-person shopping experiences.

It is important to note that growth encompasses more than just the efforts of product teams. It also includes other crucial activities such as marketing, advertising, and merchandising. The distinction lies in the specific activities that product managers carry out to drive ecommerce growth, which significantly contributes to the overall growth of the company.

In fact, the majority, if not all, of the tactics employed by product managers for growth are closely coordinated and done in partnership with other functions within the organization. This collaboration is crucial in order to achieve impactful results.

Roles involved in ecommerce growth

Product managers have the responsibility of overseeing the overall strategy and direction of a product or a group of products throughout their entire lifecycle. They collaborate closely with cross-functional teams to identify customer needs, create product roadmaps, and prioritize features using market research and feedback.

Product managers are responsible for managing the entire product development process. This includes coordinating product launches and evaluating the performance of the product in relation to the business goals.

On the other hand, project managers have the responsibility of effectively planning, executing, monitoring, and closing a specific project in order to ensure its success. They collaborate closely with project teams to ensure that projects are completed within the designated time frame, adhere to the allocated budget, and fulfill the project objectives.

Project managers are responsible for overseeing project timelines, managing resources, and mitigating risks throughout the entire project lifecycle.

Product managers focus on the big picture of a product's development and lifecycle, while project managers are focused on the successful completion of a specific project within a given timeframe and budget.

There may be some overlap between the two functions, particularly in smaller organizations, where a product manager may also take on project management or scrum responsibilities. This is not optimal and the functions need specific attention as early as possible.

In general product managers own the "What" and "Why" of the product, initiative or experiment and project managers own the delivery - the When and How.

Together they can deliver complete products, features and enhancements which are well thought through, justified, delivered, launched and tracked.

- Product manager: Why & What
- Project, program, scrum: How, When

For example, the Product Manager (PdM) will conduct an investigation into the current challenges related to product retention. They will generate ideas and design experiments to implement various improvements or additional features aimed at increasing retention.

With well defined design and requirements the Project Manager or Scrum Master will guide the team to build and deliver the product to ensure the expectations are being met in the short and long terms.

The product manager leads and oversees the entire product creation cycle from inception to launch with different stakeholders including engineering and development, marketing, customer service, analytics, business and more.

Does a product manager's role end with the launch?

Ultimately the product manager should remain responsible for making sure the products they launched, or own continue growing and improving on metrics important to the business.

In some organizations the product managers' work ends with the launch and the product goes into maintenance mode. This is not optimal and results in low or stagnant growth.

Working on The Why

What are the reasons for launching a new product or feature?

Why would you want to make changes to something that appears to be functioning well?

In the movie "The Matrix," Mr. Smith repeatedly asks Neo, "Why do you get up, Mr. Anderson? Why?"

Yes, Neo is an exceptional individual who assumes the immense responsibility of leading the entire human race towards liberation from the Matrix, fostering their growth and development.

Growth professionals wake up every day for the same reason. To save their product and company from stasis, and decline.

The life of growth professionals and teams is characterized by their belief in the possibility of something better and their determination to keep going even when experiments don't yield the expected results.

Growth masters learn from every experiment and experience, to do better on the next one. They understand that defeat is inevitable, and understand they need to consistently, and repeatedly pick themselves up and try again. And in many cases influence their team members to continue towards the goals.

Jeff Bezos consistently emphasizes the importance of maintaining a Day 1 mentality to his employees.

He also highlights that the consequence of not experiencing growth is stagnation, which ultimately leads to stasis, which is when organizations begin to decline and be replaced!

The concept of "why" also extends to brand new products, strategies, opportunities, and tactics, which is a focus in this book.

Expanding the business both at the top and bottom level.

The term "top" refers to strategic growth initiatives, while the term "bottom" refers to existing feature-focused growth. Both components are necessary for a healthy growth system.

As a product manager, it is important for us to always prioritize growth, regardless of whether our role is aligned with the strategic or tactical aspects of the business.

I recommend reading Marty Cagan's book "Empowered" to learn more about what product managers can or should be doing for the organizations they serve.

Let's now discuss the specific roles and titles of growth practitioners.

Growth product manager

A Growth Product Manager is a specialized role in product management that specifically focuses on driving user growth, engagement, and retention for a product or service. The main objective is to find ways to grow the user base and boost the product's adoption rate. Additionally, improving user experience and satisfaction is also a key focus. Some important responsibilities of a growth product manager include:

Developing a growth strategy: Identifying target audiences, understanding user needs, and defining objectives to drive user acquisition, engagement, and retention.

Data analysis and insights: Analyzing user data to identify trends, patterns, and opportunities for growth. This includes monitoring key performance indicators (KPIs), conducting cohort analysis, and using other analytics tools to inform decision-making.

Experimentation and optimization: Designing, implementing, and analyzing A/B tests and experiments to optimize product features, user interfaces, messaging, and other aspects of the product experience.

Cross-functional collaboration: Working closely with various teams, such as engineering, design, marketing, and sales, to develop and execute growth initiatives. This often involves aligning goals and ensuring smooth communication across teams.

Feature prioritization and roadmapping: Determining which product features or improvements should be prioritized to maximize growth opportunities, and creating roadmaps to guide the product's development.

User acquisition: Collaborating with marketing teams to design and execute user acquisition campaigns, and specifically focus on converting the traffic marketing brings in into customers.

User onboarding and retention: Ensuring a seamless onboarding experience for new users, as well as employing retention and engagement methods, such as personalized content or in-app messaging.

Monitoring and reporting: Keeping stakeholders informed about the progress and impact of growth initiatives by regularly tracking and reporting on relevant metrics.

Growth product managers combine skills from product management, data analysis, marketing, and user experience to drive the growth and success of a product or service.

They are constantly seeking ways to improve the product and achieve business objectives, making data-driven decisions and adapting to changing user needs and market trends.

Growth hacker

A growth hacker is a marketing professional who thinks outside the box and specializes in using creative and unconventional methods to achieve rapid growth for a company.

Growth hacking involves experimenting with various strategies and tactics to identify what works best to drive growth for a product or company.

Unlike traditional marketers who may focus on long-term brand building and customer engagement, growth hackers often prioritize short-term results such as increasing website traffic, acquiring new customers, or improving conversion rates. They also tend to rely heavily on data-driven decision-making and are skilled at leveraging technology and automation to scale their efforts.

Some common growth hacking tactics include viral marketing, search engine optimization, social media marketing, email marketing, and paid advertising. The goal of growth hacking is to find low-cost, high-impact solutions to help a business rapidly grow its customer base and revenue.

Regardless of the title for the role, the important and common responsibilities of growth focused ecommerce professionals are similar and include what we discuss in this book.

Growth Engineer

A growth engineer is a hybrid between an engineer (a software developer) and a growth hacker, and they are the first growth-focused team members in some firms.

A growth engineer is a more technical and hands-on position than a growth product manager. A product manager will often oversee a cross-functional growth team, and as an organization's level rises, several teams and product managers will report to the head of growth.

Product managers play a central role in the growth of ecommerce and retail organizations in general, and more specifically are involved to expand and improve the relationship with existing customers.

From having a pulse on the market and customers, identifying opportunities, evaluating and communicating with stakeholders, securing the budget and resources and specifying the improvement or new features and technology to overseeing the buildout, launch and monitoring post-launch the product manager is or can be involved in all of these activities. This is a role with enormous responsibility, and interestingly enough usually no direct authority over teammates they work with.

Artificial Intelligence and ecommerce

Artificial Intelligence (AI) has been in existence for several decades and has been widely utilized in the field of ecommerce. It has played a significant role in various aspects such as personalization, customer service and process automation.

Recently, there has been a rise in the use of a new form of AI known as Generative AI. This advanced technology has taken traditional AI to the next level.

Pattern matching and recognition were two of the most common applications of traditional AI in online retail. It looked at past data for trends and then made recommendations about what its consumers might like to see more of.

Generative AI distinguishes itself by utilizing historical and existing data to generate novel ideas or recommendations that may not necessarily be linked to patterns found in the original data.

For instance, products like ChatGPT, which is a language model, have the ability to process large volumes of data and generate new outputs by responding to user questions or prompts.

Open source tools like AutoGPT use Generative AI to enhance the capabilities of chatGPT. They achieve this by enabling the system to perform a series of tasks determined by the machine. As a result, AutoGPT can provide more comprehensive and detailed answers to user queries.

We are currently in the initial stages of implementing Generative AI into our work and anticipate gaining a wealth of knowledge as we progress. In the future, it is reasonable to expect that both traditional AI and newer Generative AI technologies will be utilized in the field of ecommerce.

Here are some examples:

- In customer support: Chatbots powered by language models like ChatGPT can provide customers with instant support and assistance, answering common questions and resolving issues quickly and efficiently.
- In personalization: Chatbots can use data from customer interactions to personalize the shopping experience, offering personalized product recommendations and tailored promotions based on customer preferences.
- In marketing: Chatbots have the capability to deliver personalized marketing messages to customers, taking into account their behavior and preferences. This targeted approach not only enhances customer engagement but also has the potential to drive sales.
- In feedback: Chatbots have the ability to gather feedback from customers, which in turn helps businesses gain insights into customer needs and preferences. This valuable information can then be used to improve their products and services.
- In sales: Chatbots can be used to guide customers through the sales process, helping them find the products they need as well as making transactions quick and easy.

OpenAI, being the leader in the field of Generative AI, has an App Store. Additionally, prominent ecommerce players like Klarna (specializing in payments) and Shopify (a platform provider) are integrating chatGPT functionality into their search experiences, along with several others.

Anticipate a significant increase in innovation and the introduction of new products, app stores, communities, and partnerships. It is important to recognize that change will be a consistent aspect of this evolving landscape.

Some example of how companies in the retail and ecommerce space have experimented with AI have been:

H&M: H&M uses a chatbot named "Anna" on their website to provide customers with support and assistance. Anna can answer common questions, provide styling tips, and help customers find the products they're looking for.

Sephora: Sephora uses a chatbot named "Sephora Virtual Artist" to help customers find the right products and test them out virtually. The chatbot uses augmented reality technology to allow customers to try on makeup and see how it looks before making a purchase.

1-800-Flowers: 1-800-Flowers uses a chatbot named "Gwyn" to help customers find the right flowers and gifts for their needs. Gwyn can provide personalized recommendations based on customer preferences and help customers complete transactions fast and effortlessly.

eBay: The "ShopBot" chatbot is used by eBay to assist users in finding and purchasing the items they are looking for. ShopBot can help clients identify the products that best suit their needs by making personalized recommendations and assisting them in filtering search results.

New AI, specifically generative AI, is unleashing a new generation of shopping assistants with the ability to conduct natural human conversation with shoppers and product managers are at the center of determining which AI technologies to understand and experiment with to improve their product's next-level communication with customers.

Data is (and will be) king

As research and development have shown for generative AI applications, specifically related to retail and ecommerce there are two main pieces:

- The platforms: foundational LLM models

- Training data

What is becoming apparent is that even though initially the focus was on the LLM tools and software, it's becoming more apparent that the data is even more valuable and important for the AI agents to perform well.

Data quantity and quality are the next competitive advantages of companies and every company needs to have a "data strategy" in future.

PM functional practice areas

The functional practice areas encompass the domains in which product managers exert their utmost influence and make direct contributions to the performance and expansion of the product or company.

Acquisition

Acquisition involves efforts aimed at obtaining new clients for your business, website, or app. In this role, you will collaborate closely with marketing, design, analytics, and engineering to study user behavior on your sites and devise tactics and plans to increase the pace and amount of new customers, as well as the quality of those consumers.

Converting website or app visitors into paying customers. This phase is often referred to as Conversion Rate Optimization (CRO) and falls under the purview of product teams with significant input from marketing.

Another practice, known as Product-Led Growth (PLG), involves incorporating features directly into the functionality of products. For example, if a product requires more than one person to function properly, it can be used to significantly expand the customer base. Every new user will attract additional users to the product, creating a self-sustaining cycle of growth.

Engagement

Engagement is the function that strives to keep existing consumers interested and connected with your product. Engagement is crucial because it may lead to recurring purchases that are substantially less expensive than new Customer Acquisition Cost (CAC) and boost Lifetime Value (LTV).

Part two includes many engagement tactics and strategies.

Retention

Retention actions involve two key components: understanding churn signals for your product and designing staged processes to encourage customers to continue making purchases. This can be achieved by offering deeper discounts or other benefits as the customer progresses further into the churn cycle.

Based on your understanding of customer behavior, purchasing patterns, and data from analytics, you can develop criteria to identify changes in purchase and usage behavior that may indicate a customer is likely to churn.

Based on these signals, you can take proactive measures to prevent drop-off or delay cancellations, with the hope that a certain percentage of users will continue using the service.

The Business

While it is not necessary for all product managers to be involved in business decisions, growth product managers should actively participate in the business by gaining a comprehensive understanding of key performance indicators, goals, performance metrics, and potential opportunities.

This involves actively participating in the identification and evaluation of opportunities for growth, whether it be through improving existing systems or introducing innovative ones, processes, and tools.

Business metrics and KPIs

The product manager should have a thorough understanding of key business metrics, including COGS (cost of goods sold), margins, shipping, delivery, returns, and other factors that contribute to cost evaluation and idea generation within the business.

To perform well in this role, and become empowered to contribute, product managers need to have an understanding of the business and financial situation of the organization and their products.

In many organizations business details are not provided to product managers and held close to the chest by higher level leadership and accounting departments. This puts the product manager at a disadvantage and reduces the impact they can provide on the What and Why of building and growing products.

Empowered product managers, and teams, understand the business implications of their work and as a result run more effective product organizations.

Lifetime Value

LTV or customer Lifetime Value is a metric used by companies to measure the total revenue generated by a customer over the entire duration of their relationship with the company. The lifetime value of a customer is an important metric for businesses because it helps them determine the value of acquiring and retaining customers in the long run.

LTV is mostly an estimate or aim based on assumptions in the early stages of a company's life. After a few years of operation, real historical figures may be collected to calculate LTV, and future estimates can be produced with higher probability.

To calculate LTV we can use a formula such as:

Early stage LTV = (ave. price of products) (frequency of purchases per year) (number of years customers could stay with the company).

A very basic example: Pizza delivery company

Ave price of Pizza = $20
Reasonable number of times customer can order = 12 (1/mo if they like our Pizza)
Number of years = 3

LTV = (20) (12) (3) = $720 meaning if the assumptions are correct the company can expect to generate $720 worth of revenues from each customer.

Note that this is gross revenue and we need to be looking at net revenues, at minimum including fixed costs build a healthy business.

Assuming the pizza company operates at a 50% gross margin, this means Net LTV = $360.

LTV can be used to calculate how much the company can spend to acquire a new customer, called Customer Acquisition Cost (CAC).

The ideal CAC to LTV ratio can vary depending on the industry and business model.

However, as a general rule of thumb, a healthy CAC to Net LTV ratio is around 4:1.

This means that the net lifetime value of a customer should be at least three times greater than the cost of acquiring that customer.

There is also the recovery period which is how long it will take to recoup the acquisition costs from a new customer. This is important because there is a cost to the investment made including interest, wasted resources as well as lost equity. We want to optimize for capturing the initial acquisition costs as early as possible from the customer.

Here are a few sources that provide insights into CAC to LTV ratios for different industries and business models:

According to a study by Pacific Crest Securities, the median CAC to LTV ratio for SaaS companies was 0.8, indicating that many SaaS companies were spending more to acquire customers than they were generating in lifetime value. However, top-performing SaaS companies had a CAC to LTV ratio of 1.5 or higher.

A study by McKinsey found that the CAC to LTV ratio for e-commerce companies typically ranged from 2:1 to 5:1, depending on the category of goods sold. For example, companies selling consumer electronics had a higher ratio than companies selling apparel.

From a business or product potential the potential LTV can be a key gauge into how good the idea or market for the product can be.

- If there is high LTV potential there are many more levers to pull to increase margins, profits, FCF (free cash flow) and other significant metrics.

- If LTV potential is limited the business is constrained by what it can do and has a harder time improving KPIs (key performance indicators).

- Businesses with high LTV potential are typically more valuable in the market than low LTV.

Many of the techniques and tools in Part two contribute to increasing the Lifetime Value of customers.

Transactions vs. strategy

As we explore the ways in which we can grow a product's reach, effectiveness and performance it's important to keep a balance between transactions and strategy.

Strategy is the long term map for reaching a destination, and for ecommerce the destination is maximum reach and revenue potential.

Is there a limit to LTV?

Is there an end to the range of products and services Amazon or Walmart can offer consumers? This is the exponential potential of large marketplaces and it is a potential for other companies, if there is the will and expertise to keep pushing the envelope.

As we all know Amazon started with just books, and as a direct ecommerce website. They could have stayed and become a leader in books and likely have a decent business. But that level of thinking is absent at Amazon, Walmart, Apple and other retail leaders. This is what they call day 1 mentality at Amazon, and other companies also operate with similar energy even if they don't have a name for it.

Given the wide range of product categories and customer touch points, coupled with the ever-increasing influence of technology on consumer behavior, it is evident that the potential for customer lifetime value (LTV) in these enterprises is virtually limitless.

Product managers need a firm grasp on the economics of the business and their product in order to identify and capitalize on expansion prospects.

Although the product manager may not have direct control over the budget, they are ultimately accountable for the performance of their products.

Industry knowledge and staying current

As product managers in ecommerce and retail, we need to be nimble enough to adapt quickly to the ever-shifting conditions that affect the work we do.

In addition to technical expertise, the following factors positively influence the performance of ecommerce product managers:

- Market Trends and Customer Behavior
- Competitive Landscape
- Payment options
- Logistics and Fulfillment
- Customer Support and Feedback
- Security, privacy, regulatory and legal trends and requirements
- Business Strategy and Financial Management

Given the abundance of information available on these topics, it is crucial to compile a concise list of reliable sources to effectively stay informed.

How do you stay current with micro and macro events in your industry?

Experimentation and experiment design

Experiments should be considered the foundation for growth in the role of product managers. Without a well-designed and efficient experimentation plan, our products will not be able to reach their full growth potential. Furthermore, even if they do grow, it will come at a high cost.

This topic is quite extensive, and while we can only provide a brief overview, it is important to consider and strategize the experimentation system for your product and organization.

Product managers conduct two primary types of experiments.

- Top level product experiments.
- On page/screen optimization experiments (Aka A/B testing - see part 2)

Product level experimentation:

In order to construct experiments that would rapidly and inexpensively confirm or refute the hypothesis, experimentation for products, new features, and important business activities begins with the hypothesis of opportunity. Product managers may excel in this area by creating the finest experiments.

The most effective experiments are those that are small in scale but still yield valuable and dependable data for evaluating a hypothesis and making intelligent choices.

To have a working experimentation cycle, businesses must have the right mentality and culture, a culture of experimenting. A culture that looks forward to openly recognizing and spreading the word "Experiment" A culture in which "Experiments" are designed to validate our theory rather than "Decisions." This requires support and effort from the top of the business, which is frequently where organizations fall short since investors and Wall Street don't like uncertainty, even though they all swim in it every day, and they want solid and faultless judgments from firm management. As a result, the CEO, executive teams, and boards dislike framing their activities as experiments. This is where Amazon shone under Jeff Bezos, being so unusual and disruptive that no one could catch up.

Interaction experimentation

At the level of the page/screen/interaction, a robust A/B testing and analysis system is required to create a continuous test, measure, and enhance cycle. And this is where AI can significantly improve the time management of product teams.

Experimentation culture:

One reason for highlighting this topic is that ecommerce teams primarily focus on experimenting and testing at the interaction level, rather than on the product or idea hypothesis.

While it is crucial to prioritize interaction efficiency, solely concentrating on this aspect without monitoring the performance of our overarching assumptions and hypotheses can lead to a subjective innovation environment where the opinions of the highest paid individuals (HIPPOs) dominate, often without being accurate.

The experimentation system is also dependent on the company's software and IT, which may significantly slow down the speed of experimentation as well as the rate of innovation and growth.

When designing a robust experimentation system, it is crucial to ask ourselves the question: "Are we maximizing our potential for innovation and growth?" Are we perhaps setting our expectations too low due to the limitations imposed by our systems, culture, and mindset?

How can we effectively measure and enhance this aspect of our company?

Boards of Directors should inquire about the experiments being conducted and planned by the executive teams. They should ask about the progress and outcomes of past and ongoing experiments, as well as the lessons discovered through them.

Measuring the performance of experimentation programs

Although there might not be specific mathematical formulas for higher-level program performance, you can create aggregated indices or composite metrics that incorporate multiple dimensions of performance.

Composite metrics are often derived from a combination of key metrics and factors.

For measuring composite metrics of a program we need to determine the metric and it's weight (importance or impact) as well as other attributes such as duration, frequency and even seasonality of key metrics.

Designing composite metrics for your experimentation program is an important exercise in better understanding the impact of different activities and KPIs on overall business goals. Composite metrics provide a more holistic view of how your experimentation program is performing and an important part of a product manager's collaborative work with analytics and other teams.

I'll finish this section with a note that analytics should never be a siloed team where expert data engineers come up with how the program is set up, run and evaluated in a silo.

Experimentation is a team effort and for best results highly transparent, both on positive and not-positive results.

Friction

Any obstacles or restrictions in the online purchasing process that discourage or prohibit customers from completing a transaction are referred to as ecommerce friction. Friction points can occur at any stage of the consumer experience, from product browsing through the checkout process.

Examples of ecommerce friction points

Slow page load times can be a source of frustration for customers.

Complicated navigation can discourage customers from exploring our website or other experiences.

Insufficient or unclear product information can make it difficult for customers to make informed purchasing decisions.

Hidden fees such as shipping or handling charges can surprise customers and discourage them from completing a purchase.

A complex or confusing checkout process can cause customers to abandon their cart and seek out a more user-friendly website.

Technical issues such as website errors or glitches can disrupt the online shopping experience and cause frustration for customers.

The average conversion rate impact from each additional friction point can vary depending on the specific ecommerce business and the customer experience. According to a study by Baymard Institute, each additional form field in the checkout process can cause a 4.1% decrease in conversion rates.

This means that a lengthy checkout process with many forms and fields can have a significant impact on conversion rates and revenues.

Outcome vs. output

In the context of product management, "output" and "outcome" refer to two distinct progress and achievement indicators. Both are significant, but they are distinct and should be understood independently.

- **Output:** Typically, output refers to the tangible products, features, or deliverables produced by a product team. Outputs are the final products of a development cycle.
- **Outcome:** On the other hand, an outcome refers to the tangible result that is derived from the output. It refers to the change or impact that occurs as a result of the output that was generated. The outcomes frequently align with the strategic goals of the business and the value provided to users.

For instance, a desired outcome may be "increase user engagement within the platform by 15%".

The outputs required to accomplish this outcome are manyfold and will require multiple experiments. Each experiment can be an output unit, and some large experiments will include multiple output units.

In well run product organizations, outputs are looked at and measured according to how they impacted desired outcomes, not as individual units in and of themselves.

Our unwavering focus must always be on delivering exceptional outcomes, rather than merely fixating on outputs.

This strategic approach ensures that the work being executed is effectively generating value and propelling the organization towards its overarching goals.

It also helps to prevent falling into the trap of being busy without being effective.

This means avoiding the situation where a lot of outputs, such as new features, are produced without actually achieving meaningful outcomes, such as user satisfaction, increased engagement, or revenue growth.

Product + market + customer development

As product managers we are always on the hunt for new and better ways to help our customers, products and company.

The continuous nature of the search for improvement and growth required specific skills, even mindset, attitude and personalities for successful product management.

The continuous search for growth embodies itself in several specific forma:

- Market
- Product
- Customers

The first level of inquiry is into the market. What are any known and unknown factors in the market and industry we operate in or want to enter? How do these factors impact customers, who is offering solutions for these and what is the level of innovation.

After gaps and potential opportunities have been identified, the next step is to add more details and substance on what products or solutions which could fill the gaps might look like.

Along with the above steps we are always thinking about who the ideal customers would be for this product. This starts with people already impacted by the gap in services or products, or new customer segments we need to develop and onboard.

There is extensive work involved in all these processes and multiple books and program are available only to help product managers with these. I'm including them here because the growth mindset for product managers needs to be continually fed by these processes and it's imperative for us to educate ourselves and get better at them.

Customer centricity and obsession

At the center of all product management work is the concept of the "customer".

Everything we do must start and end at the value for our customers and how we make their lives and work easier, simpler, faster, more interesting or more rewarding.

We must be truly **customer centric**, and better yet **customer obsessed**!

Customer centricity is a business philosophy and approach that places the needs, preferences, and satisfaction of customers at the center of all business activities.

To succeed and thrive, a company should prioritize understanding and meeting the needs of its customers effectively.

At Amazon, in the early days, there was always an empty chair in the meeting reserved for the customer.

Customers can be external, internal, individuals, employees, business or governments - it does not matter!

Customer obsession

Both customer centricity and customer obsession focus on prioritizing customers, although they have slightly different connotations and implications.

While customer centricity involves placing the customer at the center of business activities and making decisions that align with customer needs and preferences, customer obsession takes the concept a step further.

Customer obsession implies an intense, unwavering focus on customers that goes beyond just meeting their needs.

A customer-obsessed company doesn't just prioritize customers; it becomes entirely dedicated to exceeding customer expectations, anticipating their needs, and going to extraordinary lengths to deliver exceptional experiences.

Customer obsession often involves a deep emotional connection with customers and an unrelenting commitment to their success and satisfaction.

Steve Blank's book, Customer Discovery is a good starting point for building your personal growth program.

Jobs To Be Done

Product managers utilize various techniques to develop customer-centric products and processes, one of which is the JTBD (Jobs To Be Done) framework.

The JTBD framework serves as a guiding light in crafting user stories and use cases that revolve around the tasks customers are employing our product to accomplish. This approach leads to the development of products that are truly customer-centric, ultimately enhancing their overall experience.

"Job" of a consumer refers to the actions a person is attempting to accomplish when they engage in shopping activities.

Understanding this "job" enables product managers in retail and ecommerce to better understand their consumers and tailor their products and services to meet their requirements and expectations.

Here are some key aspects of the shopper's job while shopping:

- Shoppers often seek information to make informed decisions.
- Some shoppers enjoy (and some don't) the process of browsing and exploring stores or websites to discover new products or trends.
- Many shoppers have a budget in mind and aim to find products that fit within their financial constraints.
- In physical stores, shoppers may seek a sensory experience, including the opportunity to touch, feel, or try out products before buying them.
- Shopping can also be a social activity. Some shoppers may visit stores or shop online with friends or family members, seeking

not only products but also social connections and recommendations.

- Problem-solving is part of the shopping job. Shoppers may encounter issues or problems during their shopping journey, such as finding a specific item, resolving conflicts with a purchase, or getting assistance from customer service.
- Shopping can provide emotional satisfaction, whether through the excitement of finding a great deal, the joy of gift-giving, or the sense of self-expression through personal style choices.

Understanding the diverse jobs our customers perform to find or do what they are looking for is key to the success of product managers and owners.

Platforms and architecture

This is more on the technical side ecommerce company operations and ultimately the platform is the responsibility of engineering.

However, as product leaders we need to ensure that the platform and its architecture do not hinder our ability to effectively experiment and optimize for best business results.

The platform and architecture of your ecommerce experience is increasingly becoming a key factor in success of ecommerce, and retail in general.

Modern architectures utilize open architectures and the practice of microservices architecture (MSA) allow for the most flexibility in optimizing and improving systems. A typical ecommerce platform, specially for larger operations, needs to be updated every 5-7 years and this is a very expensive undertaking both in time, resources and finances.

Open architectures such as MSA provide more flexibility in putting an interchangeable stack of services which can more easily be exchanged when the time comes, for example in the case of the front-end (or CMS - content management system) and the headless platform concept and composable commerce.

It is important for product managers to understand the platform, its capabilities and limitations to better collaborate and plan in planning and launching new capabilities for customers.

Industry groups such as the MACH alliance (microservices, API-first, cloud-native SaaS, headless) are new industry groups working to bring a common set of standards for building the next generation of ecommerce platforms and tools.

Part Two

Tools and techniques for ecommerce growth

In Part One we went over the core pieces of the role of product managers in ecommerce companies and some other foundational skills for product managers.

In Part Two we will cover 40 different features, capabilities and tactics for instilling growth into our products. This is the ACTION phase.

A reminder that this part of the book includes 40 ideas for growth, and to reconfirm expectations:

- This is not a comprehensive list of all the options and tactics available to ecommerce and product managers on growth.
- Not all the ideas apply to every product. Every product is different with different customers and nuances, some of these techniques may not work for your product.
- This book is not a deep dive into every idea included. There are books, training and degrees on every one of these ideas.

What I am doing is recommending you consider, investigate or experiment each of these ideas for your specific products, customer base or company to determine if any of these ideas are worth experimenting.

Part Two is designed to help product professionals build a disciplined and <u>systematic way</u> to explore growth opportunities.

Roles and responsibilities

To be clear, product managers investigate and implement the functionality in all the features and capabilities listed in Part Two and the actual users will be different functional teams.

For example the actual bundling and packaging will be performed day to day by marketing and merchandising and as product manager we're not going to decide on the actual product bundles and packages. Our role post-launch is to ensure the teams have access to the tools, the tools are performing as expected technically and automated analytics are tracking the business performance of the functionality or tool.

Every function or tool needs to have initial expectations and success goals, and analytics and reporting should be performed automatically without any human interference. This means the marketing tool's performance should not really be provided by the marketing team, and for that matter for any individual role to reduce subjectivity and potential bias for any team or individual to present the results in a way to make their role or responsibility look better than it is.

Buy vs. Build decisions

In all cases of the items included in part two there is ultimately a decision to be made, to build or to buy the capabilities. This decision can apply to various aspects of the product including software, technology, services, or even physical products.

Key considerations for the "build vs buy" decision are:

Build:

Customization: If you have unique requirements that cannot be met by off-the-shelf solutions, building a custom solution may be the better option. This allows you to tailor the solution to your specific needs.

Competitive Advantage: If the solution is a core competency that provides a competitive advantage, developing it in-house may be strategic. This is particularly relevant for businesses in technology or innovation-driven industries.

Control: Building in-house provides greater control over the development process, allowing you to adapt quickly to changing requirements, fix issues promptly, and maintain ownership of the entire system.

Integration with Existing Systems: If the solution needs to integrate seamlessly with existing in-house systems or processes, building it may be more practical to ensure compatibility.

Long-Term Cost: While the upfront costs of building can be higher, in the long term, it might be more cost-effective if the ongoing maintenance and licensing fees for third-party solutions are high.

Ongoing costs: every piece of software or application built in-house will need to be maintained, monitored and enhanced over time. This means having teams with the skills to do so.

The teams can be internal employees, staff-augmentation contractors, outsourced consulting agencies, or a combination. In any of these case there are costs, time and attention needed which should be carefully assessed when deciding to build in-house.

Buy:

Time-to-Market: Purchasing an existing solution can significantly reduce the time-to-market compared to building from scratch. This is crucial when speed is essential for staying competitive.

Cost Efficiency: In some cases, buying a ready-made solution can be more cost-effective, especially for standard or non-core functionalities. Licensing fees and initial costs may be lower than the expenses associated with development.

Expertise and Support: Vendors often specialize in the solutions they provide, offering expertise and ongoing support. This can be beneficial if your team lacks the specific skills required for certain aspects of the solution.

Reduced Risk: Buying a proven and established solution reduces the risks associated with development, testing, and potential technical issues. You can rely on the vendor's track record and user feedback.

Scalability: Many third-party solutions are designed to scale easily with the growth of your business. This scalability can be a significant advantage over building a solution that may require substantial redevelopment to handle increased demands.

Maintenance and Updates: Vendors are responsible for maintaining and updating their solutions, reducing the burden on your internal resources. This can be especially important for staying current with security patches and new features.

The hybrid approach:

Often, a hybrid approach will be most suitable, combining custom-built elements with third-party solutions to achieve the optimal balance of customization, cost-effectiveness, and speed-to-market. In today's services-based and API-powered products putting together an off-the-shelf stack to start and experiment with is a good idea to run quicker experiments.

Once the idea has been validated we can consider bringing some or all parts of the solution in house but only if there are compelling reasons to do so.

Product-led Growth

The majority of the ideas, features and capabilities you will find in Part Two can be classified under the topic of Product-Led-growth (PLG).

PLG is highly popular in B2B SaaS (Software-as-a-Service) applications but also apply nicely to many aspects of ecommerce and retail.

This entire book is actually written for Product Managers to instill growth features into their products and organizations so by definition these are all product led initiatives, focused on growth.

1. Account

👉 *Account can serve as a valuable tool in establishing a personal connection with customers. It enables you to showcase an elevated awareness of their needs compared to your competitors.*

The basic ecommerce account allows customers to access their order history, update their contact information, and reset their password.

The basic ecommerce account is not designed for growth and as a result misses opportunities for both the customer, you the product managers, and the company.

Moreover, the account offers a valuable chance to collect feedback, incentivize loyal customers, motivate them to share and endorse your company with others, and gain a more comprehensive understanding of their behavior and interactions. The account provides the perfect opportunity to enjoy these advantages for both our company and our customers.

Growth-optimized accounts

A growth-optimized account provides:

For your customers:

- The basics:
  - order history
  - customer profile
- Related information on products
- Up-sell and cross sell options
- Deals and specials
- Other products and services available
- Robust help and customer service / contact methods
- Likes, favorites and update on items you've tagged
- Useful and personalized content
- What's happening and new with your company
- Personalize the UI: show what's more relevant to the customer based on what you know about them

Fo you (product manager and company)

- Deep data and insights about your customers
- Trends about how your best customers interact with you
- Receive easy feedback and recommendations from users
- Better metric performance such as higher conversion, AOV and LTV.
- Potential churn signals from your best customers.

How Account works

A customer account is actually created on the back-end server side of the ecommerce application when someone makes a purchase, this is "required" to track for financial and legal purposes and not an option.

Without this information we can not process returns, track shipments and payment and a complete accounting ledger ready for potential audits. The basic account is built and tracked based on the customer's email, phone number or both.

The key differentiator with what is referred to by customers as an Account is providing a way for the customers to access this information.

In order for customers to access their account they just need to add a password to the information they already provided to make a purchase.

The only additional step for customers is to create a password, or additional 2-Factor Authentication (2FA) means of accessing their account.

Having access to an account is also beneficial for customers so if they have a question about a purchase or return they can quickly find the information without having to contact support and potentially wait.

In fact even in case of guest purchases it's best to offer a self service way for customers to access their purchase history.

From the product manager point of view the Account can be an interface where we can learn more about customers, present valuable information to them and increase engagement.

On the financial side, increased engagement in a well designed account will lead to better unit economics on key metrics such as lowered CAC, higher purchase frequency and ultimately higher LTV.

High acquisition cost is a specially challenging side of retail with an increasing cost to acquire new customers so any positive impact on lowering CA is significant growth level.

The goal for product leaders is to move customers from transactions to a relationship, ultimately a valuable and trusting partnership.

As consumers we all know shopping for the right products is not easy. It is time consuming and often inconvenient even online because search is so difficult across the Web. A trusted retailer can save a lot of time and hassle for their existing customers.

Content

Content is a key part of personalizing the account experience for customers, and building trust along the way.

For instance, if you are selling running shoes, you can provide training videos that offer guidance on improving running techniques. Similarly, if your business revolves around skateboards, you can assist customers in enhancing their skateboarding skills.

However, it is important to not limit this valuable content to just the website. By moving such valuable resources to the customer's account, you can ensure that they truly appreciate the unique benefits they receive from your company.

Notifications and reminders play an important role in maintaining customer attention although we need be careful not to spam customers.

In general if someone has purchased a product from you in the past, sending them "useful" information once in a while will not offend most people. Note that by "useful" I mean useful for them, not just you!

Implementation considerations

When looking at implementing an optimized ecommerce account we need to consider multiple sides of the completed implementation.

Here's an example of a template from a popular ecommerce platform account.

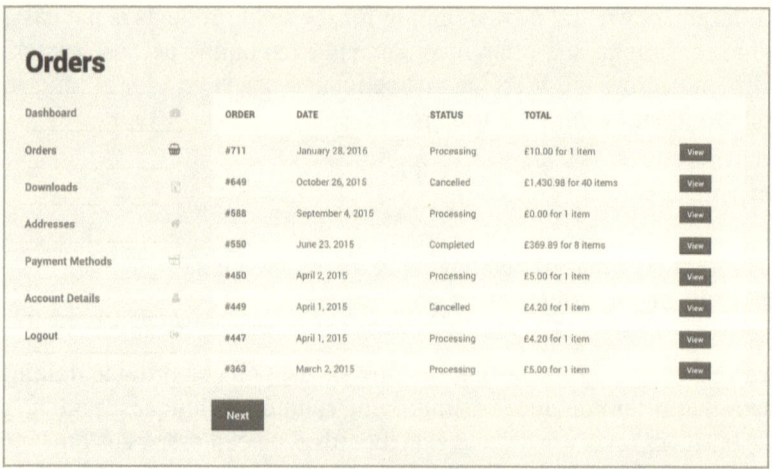

As we can see there is nothing special or exciting about this account, it's purely transactional. This is what lost opportunity looks like.

Optimizing ecommerce Account pages

On the functionality side we want to plan out user registration to users' ability to create and manage profiles, allowing customization and the addition of profile pictures, features like wishlists and favorites, notifications on discounts or restocks, personalized content dynamically curated based on user data, enhanced engagement, and relevance.

Also pay attention to design, UX and UI, as this can actually be a differentiator in modern consumers minds as well as highly mobile optimized including potentially native apps.

Also important are providing comprehensive order history and tracking details, communication preferences, personalized discounts, and loyalty programs, customer support, feedback mechanisms, and adherence to data privacy regulations.

Amazon has one of the most extensive and optimized account experiences. As we can see below there are a range of capabilities offered to customers to extend the basic account.

In fact Amazon has made the conscious decision to not allow anyone purchase from it without an account so it's clear they understand the value of the account and their results, being the largest ecommerce company in the US, speak for themselves.

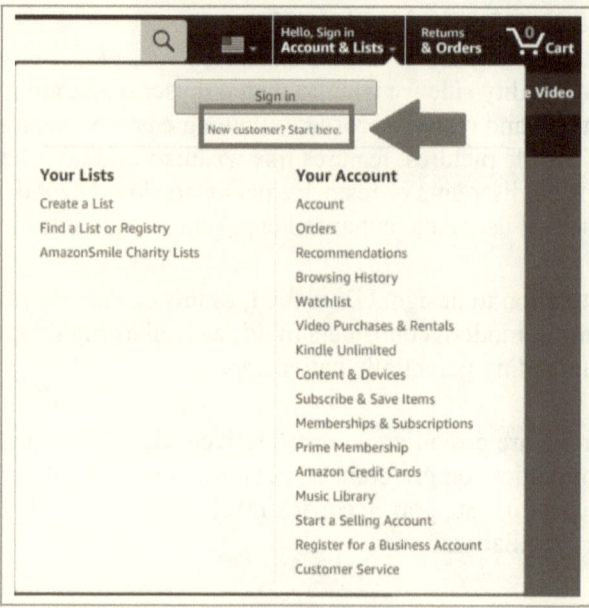

Every option here has been carefully evaluated and tested, and that continues every day. Especially on the mobile version there is limited real estate for displaying options so there is competition even inside Amazon on which features get on the menu.

Optimizing the Account is a worthwhile investment for ecommerce product leaders to unlock growth opportunities many competitors fail to capitalize on.

2. Affiliate programs

👉*Affiliate programs contribute to growth by creating a new channel for acquiring new customers without the need for advertising.*

Ecommerce affiliate programs are arrangements in which an online retailer (the merchant or advertiser) pays a commission to affiliates (publishers or marketers) for driving traffic or generating sales through their promotional efforts.

Often affiliate programs are run by marketing teams, however, the product team has an important role in ensuring the program is planned, executed and optimized along the way.

Setting up and managing affiliate programs can be time consuming and expensive, which is why a lot of retailers use affiliate marketplaces and third parties to manage the programs for them.

Some examples of successful affiliate programs are Amazon's affiliate program, known as Amazon Associates and eBay Partner Network.

An example of affiliate program managers is CJ Affiliate (formerly Commission Junction), a large affiliate marketing network that partners with retail and e-commerce companies.

Affiliate program managers can be a time saving resource for both retailers and affiliates and do have fees associated with their service.

The size of your company and its potential number of affiliates will determine if build or buy is the best option. Companies usually start with buy (using an affiliate manager) and if the opportunity size grows or they need special management controls or options they transition to the build model.

Benefits of affiliate programs

Benefits of creating an affiliate program include Increased reach and exposure, cost-effective marketing, access to new markets and third-party validation at larger scale.

There are also benefits on the Organic SEO side with additional Backlinks.

Implementing affiliate programs

When considering creation of an affiliate program we need to think carefully and objectively about the cost and effort in setting up and operating the program.

Costs include initial investment and effort, commission costs, ongoing maintenance of the program, brand reputation risk and potential brand confusion if consumers see your products on different sites at different prices. There is also the potential for fraud including click fraud or fake referrals.

Although some retail companies become affiliates of other retailers, in my experience that generally the best affiliate partners are usually pure content sites where there is low possibility of brand confusion and relationship disruption.

Influencers as affiliates

Currently some of the top affiliate marketers are called "influencers". Influencers have built audiences on social media such as YouTube, Instagram and TikTok or have their own email newsletters.

Affiliate programs are often managed by marketing teams with product managers playing an important role in helping select and set up the program as well as make sure the analytics and performance systems are established and automated to the best level possible.

3. Advertising & Retail Media Networks

☛*Selling advertising can contributes significantly to growth by providing ecommerce businesses with an additional revenue stream and help to offset the costs of running the business.*

It is possible to generate additional income by offering advertising opportunities to other complementary or relevant products on your ecommerce platform. This is especially true for marketplace businesses that have a wide range of brands and options for shoppers to choose from.

Retail media networks

The concept of Retail Media Network (RMN) is becoming more popular, and there is a growing number of tools, providers, and consultants available to assist companies with their advertising opportunities.

Ecommerce businesses can make money from advertising in several ways including display advertising, affiliate ads, sponsored content:, retargeting advertising, in-app advertising and native ads.

By exploring different advertising options and finding the right mix of advertising and ecommerce revenue, businesses can increase their profitability and drive long-term success.

Tools for building a media network

If you are looking to sell advertising on your ecommerce site, there are a number of tools that can help you set up and manage the process.

The most basic one is Google AdSense which has been providing this for many years specially for content sites. Nowadays retail companies are getting into the advertising space more and competing with content sites for eyeballs and attention.

Although AdSense is the most basic form of advertising you can offer so it should be your starting point.

Carefully see how the experience of injecting the ads into your website or app can interfere and actually harm your brand.

Tool and platform options

A starting point for setting up advertising options for ecommerce is Google Ads (previously Google AdWords). As the next step options such as Criteo can provide additional features and controls.

Advertising can and will also take new forms as retailers begin to utilize different mediums such as voice and extended reality including the metaverse.

Meta (previously Facebook) and Microsoft are building out the foundations for the future of the Metaverse, and Apple is introducing their VR headset. We can be sure that advertising will be a key part of revenue generation in the Metaverse, as it is online and in the real world.

Considerations for brands

As a brand you need to decide if you want to invest in advertising on retail sites or only focus on content-focused channels.

There are benefits for brands however it's important to be clear about the costs. Advertising costs should be carefully tracked and used in margin and ROI calculations.

For example if you are listing your products on the Amazon marketplace you will pay certain fees for access to their customer base. If you also advertise on Amazon you are paying additional fees. These fees have to come from other areas in your business, either moving from another channel such as social media or paid search or from your margins and profitability.

Historically advertising has shown significant potential for revenues for marketplace type businesses where sellers pay for advertising to stand out from the large number of competing sellers.

For single brands or retailers advertising other products on their pages has a real risk of losing the customer to a competitor for good. Advertising becomes a real option if a retailer adds a marketplace side to their business and can bring in a large number of sellers.

4. Analytics

👉*Analytics is the foundation of growth by measuring and providing valuable insights into customer behavior, product performance, and overall business performance.*

How robust and functional is your analytics and instrumentation system?

Let's start by noting that analytics is typically not a specific (vertical) feature and you might be wondering why I'm including it here as one. Analytics is actually not an option but a necessity, and it is such a critical part of growth, and it covers so much more than just Web analytics, that I am including it here again to reinforce its importance again.

At each product and feature level if your analytics are not set up properly and effectively your growth will not be optimized.

Ecommerce analytics refers to the process of collecting, analyzing, and interpreting data related to ecommerce activities with the intention to use the interpretations to make decisions.

The level of internal expertise and power of analytics tools we use is a competitive advantage in ecommerce. It can be argued that we will not be able to find a high growth ecommerce company that does not master analytics on the tool front as well as team skills.

What to measure

As we undertake setting up, running and improving our analytics systems it's important to understand the difference between KPIs and metrics.

Key Performance Indicators (KPIs) and metrics are measurements used to track and improve the performance of various aspects of a business. They do however differ in their purposes, scope, and importance.

KPIs are focused on measuring the success of specific strategic objectives or high-priority goals within an organization and are closely tied to the mission and vision.

KPIs are used to evaluate the most critical aspects of performance, which are essential for the success of the business or project.

Metrics are quantitative measures used to track and evaluate a wide range of operational aspects of a business, project, or process. Metrics typically roll up to specific organization KPI's.

Metrics in general are more descriptive than actionable, meaning they provide information about performance without necessarily guiding decision-making or improvement actions.

However, some metrics can be converted into KPIs if they become critical to the organization's success and are primarily used for monitoring, tracking, and understanding performance trends over time.

Some examples of KPIs and related metrics:

- KPI: Increase our Conversion Rate
  - Metrics: Conversion Rate, Conversion Rate by Traffic Source.
- KPI: Improve our Average Order Value (AOV)
  - Metrics: Average Order Value, AOV by Product Category, AOV by Customer Segment
- KPI: Grow our Revenue
  - Metrics: Total Revenue, Revenue by Product, Revenue by Geographic Region

Also important to consider is that KPIs can change according to organizational goals and how OKRs (Objectives and Key Results) or other methods of setting organizational targets might guide us. However, the actual metrics do not always change when KPIs or OKR change for the organization.

Another way to think about the inter-relationship of KPIs and metrics is to think of KPIs as horizontal (cross organizational goals) and metrics as vertical (specific actions or behaviors).

Platform and tools

The first tool product managers and analytics teams typically start on their analytics journey is Google Analytics (GA).

As the company grows it can outgrow GA's capabilities and need more options and controls such as Mixpanel, Segment and Heap among others.

A key determination for selecting the best tool for your company is automation and recommendation options. For example the amount of time it takes to understand the actual interaction of users with your website directly influences how your team members spend their valuable time.

Generative AI will also become a key factor in how analytics tools process data and recommend options in what's called "Idea Generation" in a way current tools are not capable of.

Mobile analytics

Different analytic tools may be needed for different touch points, for example for Websites, mobile apps and newer forms of interaction.

Mobile apps where a growing percentage of user interaction is moving are controlled mainly by Apple App Store and Google Play Store and each have their own analytics tools and capabilities.

In addition to click or tap-generated data, there is also user movement data which is useful in optimizing the screens. These tools are called heatmap software and are an additional tool to the analytics stack.

Experimentation and A/B testing

Another important aspect of product managers' involvement in analytics is the experimentation and on-page testing (called A/B testing).

Product teams work closely with analytics teams and tools to plan and track experiments on multiple aspects of user interaction with their website and apps.

Some people only think of AB testing when the topic of experimentation is discussed, which is an incomplete understanding. Full scale experimentation includes multiple views into how our products are performing from top to bottom.

Even though we have digital products our optimizations should not just focus on the user-interface (UI) side of our products. That is of course important but there is a higher, product and business level of optimization which is important.

For example if we are looking at providing an affiliate program, the top level experiments assessing the value and performance of the program are different from tool or UI related performance measures such as acquisition, engagement and conversion on different steps of the customer journey.

There are popular and free A/B testing tools including Google Optimize, Optimizely and Amplitude as well as business experimentation tools available on the market.

A key aspect of experimentation tools is how well it plays with your other tools which is determined by the ease and width of API integrations. Graphic visualization, automated notification and team collaboration capabilities also play a role in how easy the tool can deliver value to the organization.

Experiment design

In order to have a robust experimentation system we need to design experiments that deliver the data and results we need to make correct decisions.

Designing and running AB tests as well as business and product level experiments is a key skill product managers need to master. This mastery comes from education and experience in running experiments and learning from them on a regular basis.

The performance of experimentation programs can be measured by how closely experiments designed and run by a team actually deliver the optimizations and business decisions that positively contribute to business outcomes.

5. Bundles and packages

☛*Both product bundles and packages contribute to growth by encouraging customers to buy more items resulting in increased revenues, AOV (average order value), CR (conversion rate) and LTV (lifetime value).*

Product bundles refer to a group of complementary products that are sold together as a group, often at a discounted price. Product packages are typically multiple quantities of the same item sold together as one item.

Product bundles and packages can take various forms and be used across different industries, from fashion and beauty to electronics and software and have been known to increase conversion as much as 5-20%, depending on the product category and proper item selection, discount design and communication.

From the technical and inventory aspects a bundle is a collection of items curated together to form a single decision. Bundles however include multiple SKU (product IDs) which will show up in the cart individually. The discount will only be applied if all parts of a bundle are in a cart.

A package typically contains multiple quantities of a single item, but can also include multiple items put together and sold as one SKU. Customers can not break down packages into individual pieces.

Bundles

Product bundles can take different shapes and for varying purposes. Some of the more common options include:

Fixed Bundles are pre-defined bundles curated together by the retailer, for example a skincare bundle may include a cleanser, toner, and moisturizer.

Customizable Bundles where customers can pick and choose the products they want to include in the bundle from a selection of options.

Theme-based Bundles are centered around a particular theme or occasion, such as holiday bundles, or back-to-school bundles.

Starter Kits are designed for customers who are new to a product category or brand, offering a selection of essential items to help them get started.

Buy One, Get One (BOGO) Bundles provide customers savings if they purchase one product and receive another product for free or at a reduced price.

Cross-selling bundles combine complementary products from different product categories, encouraging customers to purchase additional items. For example bundling flashlights and batteries together, or engine oil and oil filter together.

Bundling as an inventory turn strategy

Bundling can be an effective strategy to get rid of unsold inventory, especially if the bundled products are complementary and the discount is attractive to customers.

Subscription bundles

Subscription boxes are a uniquely beneficial type of product bundles where customers receive a curated selection of products regularly, often on a weekly or monthly basis. The specific contents of each box may vary, providing customers with a surprise element. This model is popular in industries like beauty, food, and lifestyle.

Product groups or packages

Product packages or groups refer to sets of items that are grouped together for sale as a single unit.

This strategy is commonly used in ecommerce to encourage customers to buy multiple products at once, providing them with added value or convenience, and the retailer increased revenues due to larger orders.

Product packages can take various forms, and their composition often depends on the nature of the products and the goals of the business.

As a product manager you can:

1. Add bundle and package capability to your ecommerce application for use by your partners in marketing, merchandising and other teams.
2. Specifically for growth you will make sure the analytics are set up correctly and reporting is automated so the organization is informed and current on how the packages are performing.

To determine if a bundle or package is performing well you can use the typical product tracking and analytics for volume, frequency and conversion.

One good comparative gauge is to see if a bundle is selling better than individual items sold separately.

Bundles and also be used for a type of experimentation for combining different items together to see which ones sell better together.

Typically if the savings are enticing the bundle should sell more but if the price difference is not meaningful to customers they may decide not to purchase the bundle if they don't really need the additional items immediately.

6. Chat

☛*A robust and well attended chat program will contribute to growth by increasing conversion and potentially reducing drop offs during the purchase journey and reducing cart abandonment.*

Chat is a real-time customer support tool providing customers a way to ask questions quickly for making purchase decisions while on your website or in the app.

Benefits of chat support include real-time assistance, improved customer engagement and reduced response time. These benefits provide customers a higher sense of trust in the care a company provides to its patrons.

Live chat can also be an effective product recommendation tool in ecommerce and is certainly an area where generative AI models will shine more in the future.

There are two main types of chat applications for websites, live chat and chatbots.

Live chat

Live chat allows customers to communicate with a human customer service representative in real-time through a chat window on the company's website or mobile app.

Live chat support needs to be reliable and robust. It can be provided by your own team or outsourced to other companies reducing the requirements from your team. In either case a planned and well documented program needs to be developed with proper training and anyone engaging customers with chat.

Chatbots

Chatbots use artificial intelligence (AI) to provide automated responses to customers' inquiries. Chatbots provide automated answers to questions and in their current state are rather limited in utility. They are inherently less expensive and time consuming to purchase and maintain but still require tracking to ensure they are providing value to customers.

Key differences between live chat and chatbots include Real-time vs Automated, higher level of Personalization with live chat, product complexity where human experts can have more natural conversations with customers, availability and cost where chatbots can be available 24x7 and at no additional cost.

As a rule it is better to not offer chat capability to users than providing incomplete, low response or unprepared answers via chat.

A hybrid model can also be used where the conversation can be started with an AI powered chatbot and offer a human live chat option if the user is not happy with or can not find the information they need from the chatbot.

Chatbots and Generative AI

Chatbots and support are arguably one of the more profoundly improved capabilities from the advances in Generative AI.

As product managers we will play a key role in understanding how the new capabilities will help your organization, find and evaluate options to recommend, implement and track as well as an increased level of understanding about generative AI models, tools and capabilities.

Product managers will need to become much more informed about AI in the future.

As generative AI technology advances, chatbots are likely to improve in several ways including Natural Language Understanding (NLU), contextual understanding, conversational flow, personalization, handling ambiguity, reducing repetition and learning from user feedback.

In addition multimodal capabilities will be improved by the ability of AI agents to handle not just text but also other modalities such as images, audio, and video.

Emotional Intelligence and empathy is another promising area for improving chatbot effectiveness in helping humans along their shopping journey.

Generative AI and Shipping agents will likely have the most profound impact on retail and shopping experience.

As Bill Gates predicted in 2023, in the future people will not go to search engines and Amazon for shopping. A big, and controversial (controversial because nobody knows how AI chatbots and agents will actually evolve in the future), prediction but important nonetheless.

7. Checkout

☛*Being one of the most important parts of the ecommerce flow a well designed and optimized checkout can directly impact growth for ecommerce operations. Key metrics impacted are final conversion from intent to purchase, AOV expansion opportunities and abandonment reduction.*

Checkout is the final steps in the purchase path of customers including the cart, shipping and payment information, payment method options and order confirmation.

Product managers need to consider checkout options and strategies including:

Guest checkout

When customers go through the checkout and complete a purchase from your company you have a special opportunity to start a more long term relationship with them at that point. As mentioned in the Account chapter there are distinct benefits in having customers sign up for an account.

However, forcing customers to create accounts (basically select a password to use with their email (which you already have from the transaction) has negative effects on conversion in general. The more steps and information we force the customer to provide and go through the lower the ave. conversion rate of the checkout flow.

Guest checkout is an option some companies provide to customers. The required part of the transaction is an email address, potentially cell phone and payment and shipping info.

Benefits of guest checkout include reduced friction, improved customer satisfaction, increased sales and improved user experience.

Potential challenges with guest checkout worth considering include not capturing useful customer data resulting in less personalized experiences, limiting order tracking capabilities and a reduced ability to build longer term relationships with customers..

One-click checkout

One-click checkout is a streamlined checkout process that allows customers to complete a purchase with a single click, without having to re-enter their payment and shipping information.

One-click checkout is typically offered by ecommerce platforms that have stored customer information, such as Amazon, where customers can store their shipping and payment information to enable one-click ordering on subsequent purchases.

The goal of one-click checkout is to reduce friction in the checkout process and make it as easy as possible for customers to complete a purchase, which can improve conversion rates and customer satisfaction.

It's worth noting that one-click checkout also carries a higher risk of fraud, since customers aren't required to enter their payment information each time they make a purchase.

Single page checkout

Single page checkout is a checkout process for ecommerce websites that involves condensing the entire checkout process onto a single page.

This means that customers can complete their purchase quickly and easily without having to navigate through multiple pages to enter their payment and shipping information.

Single page checkout is designed to reduce friction in the checkout process and increase conversion rates by simplifying the user experience and eliminates the need for customers to navigate through multiple pages, reducing the risk of distraction or abandonment.

Single page checkout typically includes all the necessary fields and information required to complete a transaction, such as billing and shipping information, payment details, and order summary.

Customers can review their information and make any necessary changes on the same page, without having to navigate back and forth between multiple pages.

Single page checkout can improve conversion rates by reducing friction in the checkout process and making it easier and faster for customers to complete their purchase.

Control over checkout pages

Different checkout options need to be analyzed by product teams to provide the best performing option to customers while growing company KPIs.

In order to fully optimize the checkout flow product managers and their partners in the company best have control over individual checkout pages. This means having the ability to experiment with individual pieces of every page or step as well as adding additional features such as up-sells, recommendations and other useful features.

I usually recommend tracking and monitoring each page or section of the checkout flow individually and run experiments regularly to improve the checkout flow.

Some platforms such as the basic Shopify site do not provide control in the checkout step for optimization and for having control over the checkout flow customers need to be on the Plus program.

8. Community and customer care

☞ *A community grows a business by nurturing its customer base, increase brand loyalty, leading to new customer acquisition through word-of-mouth, and gain valuable feedback and insights for continuous improvement.*

In the context of ecommerce, a community refers to a group of customers, fans, and advocates who share a common interest or passion related to the brand or the products offered by the ecommerce business.

A community can be built through various channels, such as social media, forums, email newsletters, events, and user-generated content.

How to build a strong community

Although a community can be built inside tools and applications designed for community building and collaboration, it does not always need to be contained in an app.

The most important factor in success, or failure, of communities is the thought and care going into it on how it will "benefit the customers". If you nail this part, toll or app or just an open community will flourish and be beneficial for your customers, and in return for your product.

So focus on what values you want to provide to your community. Don't build the community to serve the company, build it to serve your customers.

Once the customer benefits have been determined, and they can evolve over time, then you can start looking at the environment and how you want to build your customer community.

The actual community can utilize one or more, but not too many, of the following options.

- Social Media Platforms such as Facebook and LinkedIn Groups
- Dedicated Community Platforms can be open-source platforms such as Discourse or custom tools.
- You can add a forum to your own Company Website and engage with customers there.

- Many professional communities today are built using Communication Apps such as Slack or Microsoft Teams.
- Reddit has also turned out to be a unique community building tool
- You can embed community features into you mobile apps if you have any.
- Email in and of itself can be a community tool. Newsletters specially are becoming popular and consumers can sign up for ecommerce and retail company emails. Just a note that pure marketing emails do not build communities unless there is a special section and content in them related to a community.
- Online events and Webinars platforms like Zoom or Webex can be used to host webinars, Q&A sessions contributing to a vibrant community.
- Local events and meetups provide members with different, and more personal, opportunities to connect face-to-face. This could include product launches, workshops, conferences, or casual meetups organized by the community or the brand.

Evaluate each of these options, or other formats suited for your customers and put a plan together on where you'll start. Remember building a community will take time and consistent attention and investment.

Building sign ups and participation

In order to get sign ups and usage, offer exclusive perks and rewards to community members, such as early access to new products, special discounts or promotions, or personalized recommendations.

In addition, providing opportunities for community members to engage with each other, such as through contests, challenges, or discussion boards contributes to engagement and growth.

Encourage community members to share their experiences and opinions through user-generated content, such as reviews, testimonials, or social media posts. When you have users creating content it's important to listen to feedback and respond promptly to questions or concerns raised by community members.

Of course, no community will be built without getting the word out so promote your community through various channels, such as social media, email newsletters, or targeted ads.

Brands may offer exclusive memberships or loyalty programs that provide members with special privileges, early access to products, discounts, or unique experiences. This can create a sense of exclusivity and encourage ongoing engagement.

Running challenges or activities within the community can be a fun way to engage members. This could include photo contests, creative challenges, or fitness challenges, depending on the nature of the community.

Hosting Q&A sessions, AMAs (Ask me Anything), or bringing in experts for panel discussions can provide valuable information to community members. This interactive format allows members to ask questions and learn from each other.

Seeking input from community members through surveys or direct feedback channels demonstrates that their opinions are valued. This can also involve members in decision-making processes, making them feel more connected to the brand.

Sharing educational content, such as tutorials, guides, or webinars, can help community members enhance their skills or knowledge related to the brand or the community's focus.

Initiating collaborative projects within the community, such as group challenges or community-driven initiatives, encourages teamwork and strengthens the bonds among members.

Building a vibrant community takes time and consistent effort. Don't get discouraged if growth is slow or there are periods of inactivity. Stay committed to your goals, keep providing valuable content, and actively engage with your members. Over time, your community will flourish and become a valuable asset for your brand.

And last by not least, partnering with and donating to charitable organizations important for your customers is a very effective way to build community

Example of vibrant retail communities

Many companies attempt at building vibrant communities, and a few do so well they become models. It's good to learn from the best and model after them, even if partially.

A couple of good ecommerce and retail companies to model after are Nordstrom, Chewy and Zappos. Each of these examples provide a master class in community building combined with customer care well worth the time to study if you decide to build a community.

9. Conversion Rate optimization (CRO)

👉 *By optimizing your conversion rate you can increase revenue per visitor, acquire more customers, and grow your business.CRO is critical for product management and growth for a variety of reasons.*

Before sending large numbers of users to a website or app it's best practice to create an experience which converts users from viewer action-taker.

The specific actions are all specifically identified and measured and the relation to other controllable factors to understand when a website or app is ready for more traffic, and how much traffic.

The initial optimization is only the start and this is a never ending process where teams, lead by product managers should be continuously engaging in actions to improve the conversion of the page, screen or messages.

The practice of CRO

This process is called Conversion Rate Optimization (CRO) and involves making adjustments to a website's design, copy, and user experience in order to increase the conversion rate of a product or service.

CRO aims to improve the proportion of users that carry out a desired activity, such as installing an app, subscribing to a newsletter, or making a purchase.

Conversion rate optimization is important because it allows you to lower your customer acquisition costs by getting more value from the visitors and users you already have.

It can also boost revenue by increasing conversion rates, which make it easier for users to complete desired actions such as making a purchase or signing up for a subscription. It has the potential to improve user experience, which is critical for growth and customer loyalty.

In order to improve conversion rate of an ecommerce site we need to break it down into individual pieces (pages or screens), and each page or screen also can be organized into specific sections.

This is the UX map which can then be used with specific test plans for each section on how to design tests to understand user behavior and improve the performance.

Designing an AB test (experiment) involves several key steps including defining the problem (or hypothesis), defining the variants, the sample size, duration and success goals.

Once the test has been designed and built we can schedule it for running and capturing data over the duration and looking for the 90% or above confidence level in selecting a winner. AB test software providers have a wealth of data on best practices well worth the read.

Heatmaps

Other ways to measure and view performance of your pages is by using Heatmaps to view the movement of users on the page.

Heatmaps can provide insight into why a specific page or block of a page is performing well or not based on what the user is seeing so it's an additional data you can use to design future AB tests.

CRO can be a complex and time consuming process and sometimes the best practice option is to hire an outside agency to handle it for you. Another advantage of hiring an agency is you don't have to actually pay for the tools which can often be costly.

10. Cross-sells and up-sells

☞ *Cross-selling and up-selling practices can contribute to the growth of a business by increasing revenue, enhancing customer retention and loyalty, maximizing purchase value, providing upselling opportunities, and improving the overall customer experience.*

Cross selling

Cross-sells are a functionality to provide recommendations to the shopper at or near the decision point to add-on related items to what they have selected in their cart.

For example if the customer is purchasing a sofa the cross sells could be matching end tables, pillows or end tables. If the shopper is purchasing a dress, cross sells could be accessories or shoes matching the dress. Virtually every product can have associated items which could be cross sold.

The reason cross-sells work is that the customer has already made a decision, or has short listed, to buy a product and is mentally more open to related items to what they have already committed to.

Cross-sells can even help the customer to complete purchase of the original product but creating a better deal overall and are frequently used on product pages, throughout the checkout process, and in lifecycle campaigns.

Cross-sells are designed in coordination with marketing and merchandising teams as well as finance to design acceptable margins.

A few situations in which cross-selling can be used effectively include During the product search process, At checkout and during promotions and sales. Basically it's best practice to test cross-sells on different pages and screens and measure the performance as results can be different for your company.

As an example Amazon offers cross-selling suggestions on product pages, suggesting related products that customers may be interested in. For example, if a customer is browsing for a laptop, Amazon may suggest a laptop bag or accessories.

Your ecommerce platform should have the ability to provide cross-sell functionality or plug-ins to add it.

As product managers you can build the case for experimenting with cross sells and ultimately help your partner teams have self service capability to run cross-sells and track performance.

Upselling

As opposed to cross selling, upselling seeks to create additional demand for products and services from the same accounts that currently purchase them, but at a lower level.

Upselling efforts are almost always led by sales, and may be driven by a specific objective for a group of accounts or individual account planning.

Enhances the customer experience and fosters loyalty.

Upsells can be effective in increasing revenue and customer lifetime value for ecommerce businesses.

Upselling is a sales technique that encourages customers to spend more money by purchasing an upgraded or premium version of the product they originally intended to buy.

When a company suggests that a customer buy a more expensive or higher-end version of a product that they are already considering or have added to their cart, this is known as upselling.

Upsells are different from cross sells in that cross sells aim to sell related items to what the shopper wants without changing the original item but upsells aim to change the selected item entirely.

Both strategies can be applied in a variety of ways, such as showcasing related products in a post-purchase email, offering bundle discounts, or featuring suggested products on a product page.

By proposing pertinent items that fit their needs, upselling and cross-selling can be used to enhance income while also enhancing customer happiness.

Effective upsell use cases

An upsell can be offered suggesting related or complementary products that the customer may be interested in.

Suggest additional products that complement the items in the customer's cart. This can increase the value of the order and encourage the customer to make additional purchases.

After a purchase is completed, an upsell can be offered suggesting related or complementary products that the customer may be interested in.

Upsells can be offered based on the customer's behavior on the website, such as their search history or purchase history.

Upsells can be used during promotions and sales, offering discounted or bundled products that complement the items that the customer is already purchasing.

11. Direct-to-consumer

👉 *Direct-to-consumer channels help growth by creating a direct, first-level relationship with customers which can be useful in ecommerce KPIs including higher margins and profits.*

Direct-to-consumer (D2C) refers to a business model where a brand or manufacturer sells its products directly to consumers, bypassing traditional intermediaries like retailers, distributors, or wholesalers.

As product leaders we might be looking at the business model of our company and identifying how it can become more efficient and profitable, even if it means adding or changing our business model.

How D2C contributes to growth

The direct customer relationship is the most valuable benefit of D2C companies. It helps companies capture more accurate information on their customers' demographics, purchasing habits, and other characteristics.

This information may be utilized to tailor advertising and create more personalized customer touch points leading to increased customer satisfaction, lead to more purchases, and solidify brand loyalty.

D2C also gives companies control over their pricing and positioning strategies, helping them to achieve and sustain their ideal margins.

With direct connection to customers, firms may obtain real-time input on their products or services, allowing for speedier iterations and improvements. This iterative process aids companies in staying competitive and meeting client needs.

Let's also address the elephant in the room on D2C financial complexities and expectations.

Many of the hot D2C brands raising hundreds of millions of Dollars in funding have crashed recently and valuation have come down significantly from the highs.

This is true and proven publicly, however I don't believe the reasons for the correction are the concept of D2C as a business model, and more of the interaction of founders with financial investors and Venture Capitalists.

Growth at negative margins (where every sale is actually a loss financially) can rarely lead to a long lasting, profitable enterprise. Growth with negative margins sometimes does result in creating massive enterprise value, if the company can continue to raise outside capital, likely Billions of dollars until the economies of scale can actually kick in.

My point in including this business model as a growth factor is to grow intentionally and measured, as in the 99% of profitable businesses do.

If your team can plan for the long term and is not looking for quick turnarounds then considering a change to, or adding a new D2C channel might be worth running some experiments to gather more data.

Examples of Direct-to-Consumer companies

Warby Parker was founded in 2010 with the goal of disrupting the eyewear industry by offering stylish prescription glasses and sunglasses directly to consumers at lower prices than traditional retailers.

In 2013, Warby Parker opened its first brick-and-mortar store in New York City (D2C does not have to only be online). Since then, the company has expanded its physical presence to over 90 stores across the United States and Canada.

Warby Parker went public in mid-2021 and reached an all-time high of $10.23 billion in November 2021. However, the company's market cap has since declined by over 80% to just over $1 Billion due to a number of factors, including increased competition from other online eyewear retailers, rising manufacturing costs and ever increasing customer acquisition costs resulting in lowering margins combined with encountering LTV limits. Warby Parker's market share in the US is in the 1-2% and they have highly established competition in the space which makes new customer acquisition more expensive.

This is where product managers can create ways to increase LTV and higher margins from their millions of existing customers.

Questions to ask when considering D2C

- Are my product and customer profile a fit for a D2C model?
- Do I have the design, production and logistics expertise needed?
- Are there reliable Third party suppliers we can use to handle parts of the operation?
- What would unit economics look like for our business?
- What experiments can I run to capture actual data if D2C is a potential fit for us?

An added note is that many companies are actually utilizing multiple distribution channels as a lead-gen option for their own D2C model.

For example companies might list a limited number of their products on marketplaces such as Amazon to create brand recognition and funnel customers from the marketplace into their own D2C channel.

12. Express sign up

👉 *Designed to reduce the amount of time and effort required from users to join a platform or service, express sign up helps growth by eliminating friction points in critical customer journey steps which can lead to major growth tailwinds.*

Express sign up typically refers to a simplified and expedited process for creating an account or registering for the website or app. Express sign up simplifies the registration process and reduces friction for the customer.

As product managers looking for growth levers, increasing account sign ups is a key tool to increase account holders and move them into the engagement cycle.

Impact on metrics

Express sign-up options can impact several key metrics for an online platform or service. Here are some of the metrics that can be influenced by the implementation of express sign-up:

Conversion Rate can potentially increase the conversion rate, as they lower the barriers for users to create an account or sign up.

User Registration Rate can improve due removing friction in creating an account.

Higher user engagement rates as users get quicker access to the platform's features.

Abandonment Rate can be lowered during the registration or checkout process.

Express sign-up methods expedite the process of getting new users to their first interaction with the platform.

Simplified registration processes can lead to higher user satisfaction, as users appreciate platforms that value their time and make it easy to get started.

Express sign-up options

There is an increasing number of options for offering express sign up to users. In addition to social channels new interaction options are also coming into the fold. Let's look at some of the options:

Users can sign up using their existing social media accounts, such as Facebook, Google, Twitter, or LinkedIn.

Express sign up (and sign in) involves a single button click to sign up, often accompanied by minimal required information (usually just an email address).

Users enter their mobile phone number, receive a verification code via SMS, and enter that code to complete the sign-up process.

On devices that support it, users can use their fingerprints, facial recognition, or other biometric methods to authenticate their sign-up or log-in.

There are also other Third party sign in aggregators which can manage multiple options for the company with less time needed to implement and maintain each option. to look into. (The buy option)

Single Sign-On (SSO)

SSO allows users to use one set of credentials to log in to multiple applications or services.

QR Codes or NFC Tags

In some cases, users might be able to scan a QR code or tap an NFC tag to instantly register for a service.

All of the express registration options covered can help improve growth. I recommend exploding each one for your product and take advantage of the benefits. An added benefit is if you do implement any of these options they can be used in additional products or across different channels.

13. Extending Reality

☛ New ways of letting shopper see or experience products before they buy them contribute to growth by increasing conversion, reducing returns and a heightened brand value. We are only at the beginning of this experience revolution and the companies with the most experiments will be the winners of tomorrow's retail.

One of the most transformative ways technology is starting to change human experience is by combining our physical reality with computer generated experiences.

Product managers should lead the ideation, design and implementation of these experiments.

Extended Reality (XR) is the realm of using technology to extend the experience and feel of reality beyond the 2 dimensional Web and even the physical experience. XR includes virtual reality (VR), augmented reality (AR) and mixed reality (MR).

According to research by MarketsandMarkets, the market size of all extended reality technologies combined is expected to reach USD 125.2 billion by 2026, at a compound annual growth rate (CAGR) of 30.6% between 2021 and 2026.

Augmented Reality (AR)

AR technology overlays digital content onto the physical world, allowing customers to visualize products in a real-world setting before making a purchase.

Augmented Reality (AR) is transforming the way customers interact with products and services in e-commerce.

Some examples of how AR is being used in e-commerce include,

With virtual try-ons AR allows customers to virtually try on clothes, footwear, accessories, or makeup, providing a realistic representation of how the products would look on them.

With furniture placement AR helps customers visualize how furniture and other home decor items would look in their living spaces.

Some of the best examples of AR in ecommerce include:

IKEA Place allows users to virtually place furniture and home decor items in their living spaces and help customers visualize how the products would fit and look in their homes.

Sephora Virtual Artist enables customers to virtually try on makeup products, such as lipstick shades, eyeshadow, and foundation, using their smartphone camera.

Warby Parker Virtual Try-On uses AR technology to allow customers to virtually try on glasses and sunglasses.

Nike Fit uses AR and computer vision to measure users' feet and recommend the right shoe size.

Mixed Reality (MR)

Mixed reality (MR) is a technology that blends the real world with the virtual world, allowing users to interact with both simultaneously.

MR is different from augmented reality (AR), which only overlays virtual objects onto the real world, and virtual reality (VR), which completely immerses users in a virtual environment.

MR is still in its early stages of development, but it has the potential to revolutionize many industries, including ecommerce. For example, MR could be used to allow customers to:

The Microsoft HoloLens is a prime example of MR technology. It is a headset that blends holograms with the real world, allowing users to interact with digital content in a three-dimensional space. Applications range from gaming and education to professional training, industrial design and retail.

Virtual reality (VR)

Virtual Reality (VR) technology can be used to provide a more immersive and interactive shopping experience for customers.

VR technology creates a simulated environment that can be explored and interacted with using specialized equipment, such as VR headsets.

Some examples of VR applications for ecommerce include:

Virtual showrooms allow customers to explore virtual showrooms and visualize products in a more immersive and engaging way, such as seeing how furniture will look in a room or how a car will look in a virtual garage.

Virtual try-on allows customers to try on virtual versions of clothing, accessories, and makeup in a realistic and interactive way, helping them visualize how the product will look and fit before making a purchase.

Interactive product demos allow customers to interact with and explore products in a more engaging and realistic way, such as seeing how a new piece of technology works or how a new appliance can be used in the kitchen.

By using VR technology to provide a more immersive and personalized shopping experience, ecommerce businesses can differentiate themselves from competitors and drive long-term success.

VR technology is still relatively new and requires specialized equipment, which may limit its adoption among some customers but several companies are experimenting with utilizing VR in their customer touch points.

The Metaverse

Metaverse: The term "metaverse" refers to a collective virtual shared space, merging physical and virtual reality.

In a metaverse, users can seamlessly move between different virtual experiences and worlds.

The metaverse is often imagined as a more complex and integrated version of the internet, where virtual environments, social interactions, commerce, entertainment and high on the business priority list, shopping converge.

Several companies and platforms have been working toward creating elements of a metaverse but a full-fledged metaverse is still an evolving concept.

The Facebook Metaverse, announced by Meta in 2021, is part of the company's long-term vision for the future of the internet.

Mark Zuckerberg, the CEO of Meta, described the Metaverse as the next big computing platform, following the transition from the desktop to the web and then to mobile devices.

What's next

While we mostly have heard about AR and VR in commerce and consumer experiences, we're only at the beginning of the evolution of these technologies and most people do not understand what impact XR will have on human life in the future.

Keeping an open mind and being open to experiment are key to staying relevant for ecommerce and retail product managers who will be introducing most of these technologies to their organizations and customers.

14. Fit and size

👉 *Fit software uses a variety of data points, including measurements, body type, and style preferences, to provide personalized size recommendations and help customers make informed purchasing decisions contributing to improved KPIs.*

Fit software for ecommerce refers to tools and technologies that help customers find the right size or fit for clothing and apparel items when shopping online.

Fit and size options

Virtual try-on technology allows customers to see how clothing items will fit on their body using augmented reality or 3D modeling

Size recommendation tools use data on body measurements and size charts to provide customers with personalized size recommendations.

Fit preference tools allow customers to indicate their style preferences, such as how they like their clothing to fit or how they prefer the length of a garment.

Fit reviews allow customers to share their own experiences with the fit of a particular item, helping other shoppers make informed purchasing decisions.

Impact on returns

One of the biggest challenges ecommerce businesses face is the high rate of returns due to customers receiving items that do not fit properly. By providing fit software that helps customers find the right size and fit for clothing items, ecommerce businesses can reduce returns and associated costs.

Customers who receive items that fit properly are more likely to be satisfied with their purchase and more likely to become repeat customers.

Ecommerce businesses that use fit software to provide a better shopping experience for their customers can enhance their brand reputation and stand out in a crowded marketplace. By reducing returns and improving customer satisfaction, fit software can help ecommerce businesses increase sales and profitability.

3D scanning

3D is another type of fit measurement and can be beneficial in a number of ways:

Provide highly accurate measurements of a customer's body, which can be used to provide personalized size recommendations for clothing items.

Possibly one of the most interesting applications of 3D will be combining 3D body scans of customers to virtually try on apparel, shoes and other products. Still in the research phase, this would provide a significant improvement to the current ecommerce experience of images or even 3D product carousels.

Another interesting application is to use 3D scanning to create customized products that fit a customer's specific body shape and size.

15. Gamification

☞ *Gamification contributes to growth by making a customers experience and relationship more "sticky". Stickiness is one of the key habit forming elements of product design. increasing engagement for existing customers as well as acquiring new customers and improving ecommerce KPIs.*

Gamification is a technique that involves using game concepts and elements to entertain users and influence their behavior. Gamification is based on the Action-Reward psychology all humans, and even non-human animals operate on.

Specific actions result in rewards creating a potentially endless cycle of interaction within which specific steps can lead to purchase actions.

Gamification can take various forms, such as loyalty points, badges, challenges, contests, rewards, competitions, and personalized experiences and can be integrated at different stages of the customer journey, including product discovery, browsing, checkout, and post-purchase.

Ultimately, the goal of gamification is to enhance the shopping experience and increase customer engagement, promote loyalty and retention.

Loyalty programs that offer rewards or exclusive perks to customers for completing certain actions or spending certain amounts can create a sense of achievement and encourage repeat purchases.

Running contests or giveaways that encourage customers to share their experiences or engage with the brand can create excitement and encourage participation.

Interactive product experiences, such as virtual try-ons or product customization tools, can create a sense of playfulness and encourage exploration.

Encouraging customers to share their purchases or experiences on social media can create a sense of competition or social validation.

Drawings and contests are some forms of gamification used in ecommerce effectively.

Gamification options

When designing gamified experiences for ecommerce, we can use a variety of features that enhance user engagement and provide a sense of accomplishment, including points system, badges and achievements, leaderboards, virtual currency, progress bars, challenges and missions, spin-to-win wheels, quizzes and trivia, leveling up, unlockable content, time-limited challenges, social sharing, custom avatars or profiles, augmented reality (AR) Interactions, mystery boxes or surprise rewards

As you can see there are many ways to engage customers in some form of gamification process. We need only one of these to work to provide measurable value but finding that option will take careful research and experimentation as well as experience in how the feature would work with your customers and your products.

Examples of gamified ecommerce

Lego's is a good example of gamification where their website and apps often feature interactive games and challenges that involve building virtual Lego structures. These games promote engagement and creativity, aligning with the brand's core values.

16. Loyalty programs

☛ *Loyalty programs can have a major contribution to your ecommerce business growth helping with more frequent visits and purchases, potentially larger AOV. Ultimately the LTV is the most benefited metrics from loyalty programs.*

Loyalty programs are custom design membership programs designed to offer customers incentives or rewards for making repeat purchases or taking other actions that benefit the business, such as referring new customers or sharing feedback on social media.

One of our main jobs as product managers is to encourage customer loyalty, increase customer lifetime value, and retain customers over time.

A good example of loyalty programs is in the coffee business with Starbucks.

The Starbucks Rewards program is a successful gamification example of customer loyalty. The program offers stars and points to customers, which can be collected over time and redeemed for free drinks and menu items.

VIP programs

VIP programs go hand in hand with loyalty programs and offer benefits beyond the basic loyalty program benefits including:

- Cash back and discounts
- Loyalty points and rewards
- Exclusive Discounts and Offers
- Personalized Recommendations
- Priority Shipping
- Dedicated Customer Support
- Exclusive Access to Limited Edition Items
- Invitations to VIP Events
- Extended Return Periods
- Customization Options
- Early Access to New Features and products
- Birthday Rewards
- Exclusive Content.

Tiered VIP Memberships

If you offer a VIP program you can also build a tiered benefit program to service customers with a higher level of attention and personal touch.

Example of loyalty and VIP plans

Amazon Prime and the Costco membership are the top loyalty level programs in the US among hundreds of other examples.

Another level of loyalty is associated with company credit cards including the Apple card.

Customer loyalty is one of the hardest feats to achieve in ecommerce so experimentation and investment in finding the right program for your customers is usually rewarded if the program is designed, launched and supported properly.

17. Marketplace

👉 *For companies a marketplace's main benefit is not having to carry inventory for products they sell. Inventory acquisition, management and replenishment is a complex and ongoing process so not having to do this work is a major benefit for marketplace owners. In addition you can expand into other product categories with less effort so that's another growth opportunity for marketplace owners.*

Marketplaces bring buyers and sellers of different product categories together under one umbrella and provide several key benefits to both sides.

For marketplace sellers the main benefit is not having to invest as much into customer acquisition and all the functionality and infrastructure of running an ecommerce operation. As an ecommerce brand or retailer listing products on established marketplaces can provide a new source of growth for products.

There are two main options when considering marketplaces:

1. List your products on other marketplaces.

This is the most common choice for ecommerce brands as it requires the least amount of work and investment.

2. Set up your own marketplace (standalone or in conjunction with your own website or app)

Setting up your own marketplace can be a complex endeavor but if done with proper planning, analysis and expectations it can bring significant value to the business.

Identifying and analyzing options along with the overall organizational impact and designing experiments to test assumptions is what product managers are tasked to do. In addition, following through with the implementation teams for completion, then tracking and growth is the continuation of product manager's work.

Listing products on popular marketplaces

In the USA Amazon, eBay, Walmart, Etsy are some of the largest and most popular marketplaces.

Listing on different ecommerce marketplaces comes with its own set of advantages and challenges requiring extensive education and time investment on each.

There are many resources available on marketplace strategy and growth and the coverage requires books on each one, specially Amazon which has grown so large and complex it really does require specialization.

In this specific case the complexity is the reason there are many marketplace agencies helping companies in launching and managing their marketplace initiatives.

It is a good idea to become informed about the role marketplace agencies play if you plan to explore either marketplace option.

Creating your own marketplace

In addition to or in place of listing your products on marketplaces you can also set up your own marketplace.

And of course you can also start your own ecommerce marketplace to compete with the big players in specific niche product categories.

Setting up your own marketplace can be a complex endeavor regardless which option you pick, so think carefully and experiment before making long term decisions and investments.

Of course having existing scale in customers is a major advantage for larger retailers many of whom are experimenting with their own marketplaces.

For smaller businesses a group or association marketplace can be a good potential to get closer to customers and share in the cost of launching and running a marketplace in verticals such as jewelry and furniture.

In addition to the traditional marketplaces the top social apps such as Meta (Facebook) are also options for ecommerce.

Commerce Manager is a platform to manage your catalog and sales on Facebook and Instagram.

Anyone can use Commerce Manager to create and manage a catalog, which holds all the items you want to promote on Facebook and Instagram. You don't need a shop to use Commerce Manager. However, if you sell physical products, you can choose to set up a shop on Facebook, Instagram or both. This creates a commerce account for you and unlocks additional tools in Commerce Manager.

Also important in this case is that Meta now requires all stores to use their own checkout, called Checkout with Facebook and Instagram.

You can also set up to sell products on Commerce Manager directly through Shopify but still need to use the Checkout with Facebook and Instagram for payments.

Options and requirements for each marketplace can change at any time so this is just a moment-in-time update. When you are ready to investigate any marketplace program a fresh review is required.

18. Mobile apps

☛ *Native mobile apps can contribute to growth by providing a more personal and higher performing experience for shoppers.*

When considering adding mobile apps to web-based ecommerce we have to consider the size of the company, target audience, budget, and overall business goals. And pros and cons need to be carefully weighed.

I know of established retailers and ecommerce companies who after years of operating mobile apps are re-considering keeping the apps since a small percentage of their customers use the apps.

However, if you can build some unique experiences in the app which are not possible on mobile web, the uniqueness factor can actually become sticky enough to bring more customers to your app.

One of these examples is using Augmented reality (AR) or gamification into the app.

The design of these features can be expensive but you may also be able to find pre-build pluggable features to experiment with without major expense and time investment.

On the other hand, if all we're doing in the mobile app is copying the mobile Web experience then we're not giving the customer much incentive for the added effort of downloading and keeping our app on their devices.

For certain ecommerce players such as marketplaces, discover and cross-brand shopping and large retailers and brands having a native mobile apps can reap significant rewards beyond a Website.

And in some cases including AR, VR and livestreaming the technology used is beyond availability on the Web so mobile apps are the only way to provide true benefit to customers.

Some examples of successful mobile apps for ecommerce and retail companies are:

Amazon: The Amazon mobile app allows users to browse and purchase from their vast product catalog, access personalized recommendations, track orders, and manage their account.

eBay: The eBay mobile app provides a platform for users to buy and sell items, place bids, and manage their accounts. The app makes it easy for users to search for products, compare prices, and track their purchases.

Sephora: The Sephora app allows users to shop for beauty products, access personalized recommendations, and join their Beauty Insider loyalty program. The app also offers features like augmented reality makeup try-ons and beauty tutorials.

19. Notifications and Reminders

👉 *Notifications and reminders play a crucial role in ecommerce for keeping customers engaged, informed, and motivated to interact with your platform.*

Proper notifications, with the correct content and timing can significantly benefit your interaction with customers and lead to additional purchases.

Here are some common types of notifications and reminders:

Order Notifications

Sent immediately after an order is successfully placed, confirming the details of the purchase.

Sent when the order is shipped, including tracking information and estimated delivery date.

Sent once the order has been successfully delivered to the customer's address.

Transactional Notifications

Sent to confirm successful payment for an order.

Sent when a refund or return request is processed, keeping customers informed about the status of their request.

Sent to remind customers about items left in their cart without completing the purchase, often including incentives like discounts to encourage completion.

Product Updates

Notifying customers about the latest products added to your inventory.

Alerting customers when a previously out-of-stock item becomes available again.

Personalized Recommendations

Suggesting products based on a customer's browsing and purchase history.

Notifying customers when items on their wishlist are on sale or running low in stock.

Engagement and Loyalty

Updating customers about their loyalty points, rewards, and upcoming benefits.

Sending personalized messages with special discounts or offers to celebrate milestones.

Review Requests

Encouraging customers to leave reviews for products they've purchased.

Inviting customers to share their feedback about their shopping experience.

Shipping Updates

Informing customers about any unexpected delays in the delivery process.

Notifying customers when their package is out for delivery and when it has been delivered.

Post-Purchase Follow-ups

Requesting feedback from customers to improve the overall shopping experience.

Suggesting complementary or upgraded products based on their recent purchases.

These notifications and reminders can be delivered through various channels, such as email, SMS, mobile app push notifications, and even social media platforms, depending on your customer preferences and engagement strategies.

The key is to strike a balance between helpful updates for the recipient while not overwhelming customers with too many notifications.

20. Partnerships and private label

👉 *Although many of the partnership options fall under the wings of marketing it's often the product leader which brings up the options to collaborate with and ultimately owns the delivery, success and ultimate impact on the business from these initiatives.*

Partnerships in ecommerce refer to collaborations between two or more businesses that aim to achieve mutual benefits.

By creating mutually beneficial partnerships you can grow your KPIs faster, and less expensively than you can alone.

Partnerships that product managers and owners are typically different from marketing partnerships.

Forms of partnerships

Co-branding: Co-branding involves two businesses working together to create a joint product or service that combines their brands and expertise. This can help to increase brand awareness and customer loyalty for both businesses.

Cross-promotion: Cross-promotion involves two businesses promoting each other's products or services to their respective customers. This can help to increase exposure and reach new customers.

Referral programs: Referral programs involve two businesses incentivizing their customers to refer new customers to each other. This can help to increase customer acquisition and retention for both businesses.

Co-branding

Co-branding is a marketing strategy that involves two or more brands working together to create a new product or service.

In co-branding, each brand brings its own unique strengths and assets to the partnership to create something that is more valuable and appealing to customers than either brand could create on its own.

Co-branding can take many different forms, including:

Product partnerships: Two or more brands collaborate to create a new product that combines the features and benefits of each brand.

Event sponsorships: Brands can partner to sponsor events or causes that align with their values and target audiences.

Co-marketing campaigns: Brands can collaborate on marketing campaigns to promote a shared message or theme.

Co-branding can be beneficial for both brands involved in the partnership.

Increase brand exposure: By partnering with another brand, you can tap into their audience and increase your brand's exposure to new customers.

Expand product offerings: Co-branding allows brands to expand their product offerings by creating something new and unique that appeals to a wider audience.

Build brand trust: Co-branding can help to build trust with customers by associating your brand with another trusted brand.

Referral programs (close relative to Affiliate programs)

Referral programs are marketing strategies that encourage customers to refer their friends or family members to a business in exchange for a reward or incentive. Referral programs can be effective ways for businesses to attract new customers, increase customer loyalty, and generate positive word-of-mouth marketing.

Referral programs typically involve the following steps:

Setting up the program: The business sets up a referral program with clear rules and rewards for customers who refer others.

Encouraging referrals: The business promotes the referral program to its existing customers through email, social media, or other channels.

Referral submission: Customers submit their referrals through a specific link, code, or form provided by the business.

Rewarding referrals: When a referred customer makes a purchase or takes a specific action, both the referrer and the referred customer receive a reward or incentive.

Referral programs can take many different forms, including:

Discounts or coupons: Referrers and referred customers receive a discount or coupon code for their next purchase.

Points or rewards: Referrers and referred customers earn points or rewards that can be redeemed for products or services.

Cash or gift cards: Referrers and referred customers receive cash or gift cards for participating in the program.

Exclusive partnerships

Exclusive partnerships in ecommerce are agreements between two or more businesses to work together to create a unique product or service that is only available through their partnership. In an exclusive partnership, the partners agree to work together exclusively and not collaborate with any other partners in the same industry.

Exclusive partnerships can take many different forms, including:

Product development: Two or more businesses collaborate to create a new product that combines the strengths and capabilities of each business. For example, a technology company might partner with a fashion brand to create a line of smart clothing.

Distribution agreements: A manufacturer partners with a retailer or distributor to exclusively sell its products. For example, a beauty brand might partner with a specific retailer to exclusively sell its products in-store or online.

Co-marketing campaigns: Two or more businesses collaborate on a joint marketing campaign to promote their products or services. For example, a sports equipment company might partner with a beverage company to create a joint marketing campaign for a sporting event.

Exclusive partnerships can be beneficial for businesses in many ways, including:

Increased exposure: Exclusive partnerships can help businesses reach new audiences and increase their brand visibility.

Unique product offerings: Exclusive partnerships can help businesses create unique products or services that are not available elsewhere in the market.

Competitive advantage: Exclusive partnerships can give businesses a competitive advantage over their competitors by offering something that no one else can.

Private labeling

Private labeling, also known as white labeling or private branding, is a business model in which a company produces products or services that are sold under the brand name of another company.

In private labeling, the manufacturer creates a product and sells it to a retailer, which then sells the product under its own brand name, rather than the manufacturer's brand name.

For example, a grocery store might sell a brand of cereal under its own brand name, even though the cereal was actually produced by a manufacturer. The manufacturer produces the cereal, but the grocery store sells it under its own brand name, which is printed on the packaging.

Benefit of private label programs

Private labeling can be beneficial for manufacturers, retailers as well as consumers.

Manufacturers can benefit from increased sales and revenue, as well as a more diversified customer base.

Retailers can benefit from being able to offer products under their own brand name, which can increase customer loyalty and help differentiate them from their competitors.

And consumers typically benefit from receiving the same or near-same quality products as the brand name but at lower prices.

Private labeling can be a good strategy for businesses, as it allows them to differentiate themselves from competitors by offering unique products under their own brand name.

By offering private label products, ecommerce businesses can increase customer loyalty and attract new customers who are interested in their unique offerings.

Details to keep in mind for private label programs

Some points to keep in mind if you consider a private label program:

Identify your target audience: Identify your target audience and understand their preferences, needs, and willingness to pay for private label products.

Research manufacturers: Research manufacturers that can produce high-quality products at a reasonable cost.

Select products: Select products that align with your target audience's preferences and needs. Consider factors such as price, quality, uniqueness, and competitive landscape.

Develop branding and packaging: Develop branding and packaging that align with your brand identity and target audience.

Price your products: Price your products competitively based on factors such as production costs, competitor pricing, and perceived value.

Launch and promote your private label products: Launch your private label products and promote them through your website, social media channels, and other marketing channels.

Monitor and adjust: Monitor the performance of your private label products and adjust your strategy as needed based on customer feedback, sales data, and market trends.

Private label products can offer several benefits for businesses, including:

Increased profit margins: Private label products can be sold at a higher profit margin than branded products, as the manufacturing costs are generally lower.

Differentiation: Private label products can help businesses differentiate themselves from competitors by offering unique products under their own brand name.

Greater control over pricing and marketing: With private label products, businesses have greater control over pricing and marketing.

Reduced competition: By offering private label products, businesses can reduce competition from other brands and gain a competitive advantage.

Two of the most well known loyalty programs in the US are the Kirkland Signature brand by Costco and AmazonBasics from Amazon.

- Costco offers a variety of private label products under its Kirkland Signature brand, including food and beverage products, clothing, and household items.

Amazon offers a wide range of private label products under its AmazonBasics brand, including electronics, office supplies, and home goods.

21. Payment

☞ *Providing additional and easier options for our customers to purchase our products removes friction and provide support to increase growth in conversion, frequency and Lifetime value.*

Commerce can not take place without payment so the type and popularity of payment options we provide customers is one of the must have requirements.

However with so many payment options we need to start from the most popular ones and add less popular, niche options later.

For product managers different activities around payments will lead to growth, including:

- Launching new payment methods
- Maximizing payment authorization rates
- Lowering declines
- Lowering the cost of payments
- Minimizing payment disputes, defects and fraud

Ecommerce payment types refer to the different methods of payment that customers can use to make purchases on an ecommerce website. Some common ecommerce payment types include:

Credit/debit card: Credit and debit cards are the most common method of payment for ecommerce transactions. Customers can enter their card details directly into the website to complete the transaction.

PayPal: PayPal is an online payment system that allows customers to make purchases using their PayPal account balance or linked credit/debit card.

Digital wallets: Digital wallets such as Apple Pay and Google Wallet allow customers to store their payment information securely and make purchases using their mobile device.

Bank transfers: Bank transfers allow customers to transfer funds directly from their bank account to the ecommerce business.

Cryptocurrencies: Cryptocurrencies such as Bitcoin and Ethereum can be used as a method of payment for ecommerce transactions, although they are less commonly used than other payment types.

Cash on delivery: Cash on delivery allows customers to pay for their purchase in cash when it is delivered to their doorstep. This is most common in developing countries where credit cards and other types of payment are not as readily available to the population.

Installment payments: Installment payments allow customers to pay for their purchase over time, rather than in a single payment. This is covered under financing.

Methods of Payments

Credit or Debit card:

The most popular purchasing methods are credit and debit cards. Credit is extended to buyers by credit card firms like Visa, Mastercard, American Express, and Discover; they pay for the purchase price, and users pay their card balance each month.

Visa: With over 3 billion active cards worldwide, Visa is one of the biggest payment providers. Visa offers a variety of payment choices, including credit, debit, and prepaid cards, and offers payment solutions for companies of all sizes.

Mastercard: With a worldwide network of more than 2 billion cards, Mastercard is another prominent payment processor.

Discover: Discover is a payment provider with its main base of operations in the US.

American Express: Amex is a payment processor that mainly deals in credit cards but also gives business clients payment processing options.

Debit cards offer advantages such as helping with budgeting, convenience, no debt accumulation, ATM access, and fraud protection.

The importance of offering multiple payment options to increase conversions and reduce cart abandonment rates. The report suggests that offering at least three payment options can increase conversions by up to 30%.

Express payments

Express payments provide customers a quick way to select a payment method and complete their transaction, which reduces friction in the checkout flow and increases conversion.

The most common express payment options are:

PayPal is an online payment system that allows users to send and receive payments securely via the internet.

Apple Pay is a mobile contact payment system and digital wallet tool that enables customers to pay for goods and services at the point of sale using near-field communication (NFC).

Google Pay is a digital wallet and mobile payment service developed by Google.

Amazon Pay is a payment service developed by Amazon that allows users to make online payments on external merchant websites.

Alternative payment options

Bank Transfers: Money is transferred straight from the customer's bank account to the merchant's account through bank transfers.

Cash On Delivery: Customers can make cash payments for their purchases using the cash on delivery (COD) payment option. Particularly prevalent in nations with low credit card usage is this way of payment.

Cryptocurrency: A few e-commerce websites now take bitcoin as payment. For instance, the online store Overstock.com takes payments in Bitcoin, Ethereum, and other cryptocurrencies.

Financing

Although there are different types of financing in retail, the most popular form is the Buy-Now_Pay_later (BNPL) model.

BNPL services are usually provided by third-party payment providers, who partner with retailers and ecommerce businesses to offer the payment option to their customers.

The payment provider pays the retailer upfront for the purchase, and the customer then repays the payment provider in installments.

BNPL services can be attractive to customers who want to make a purchase but don't have the funds to pay for it upfront. They can also be used to spread the cost of a large purchase over a longer period of time, making it more affordable for the customer.

Both for companies and consumers, BNPL services can also come with fees and interest charges, which can add up over time and make the purchase more expensive in the long run. It's important for customers to carefully consider the terms and fees associated with BNPL services before using them.

22. Personalization

👉 *Personalization involves using past customer data and insights to create customized experiences that are more relevant, engaging, and predictive of future actions. Personalized experiences contribute to growth by increasing conversion, order and lifetime values.*

Ecommerce personalization refers to the practice of tailoring the online shopping experience to the individual preferences and behavior of each customer.

Personalization can take many different forms, including:

Personalized recommendations: use customer data to make personalized product recommendations based on the customer's browsing and purchase history.

Personalized content: personalize the content that is displayed to each customer based on their preferences and interests, such as showing different images or descriptions of products based on the customer's past behavior.

Personalized promotions: offer personalized promotions and discounts based on the customer's behavior and purchase history.

Personalized search results: personalize the search results that are displayed to each customer based on their preferences and past behavior.

Why is personalization important

Personalization is crucial for ecommerce companies to create engaging and satisfying shopping experiences for customers and gain a competitive edge in the highly competitive e-commerce world.

Ecommerce companies can use customer data to recommend relevant products and services, tailor the user interface to customers' preferences, and personalize customer service experiences using chatbots and other automated tools. By leveraging advanced technologies and customer data, e-commerce companies can create personalized shopping experiences that lead to stronger customer relationships, loyalty, and revenue growth.

Some strategies to implement personalization on your e-commerce website:

Customer accounts: As covered in Part 2, Chapter 1 accounts encourage users to create accounts to collect valuable data about their preferences, shopping history, and behavior. This information can be used to tailor content and recommendations to each user.

Personalized recommendations: Use customer data and machine learning algorithms to suggest products or content that are relevant to each user. This can be based on their browsing history, past purchases, or items in their cart or wishlist.

Dynamic content: Adjust website content, banners, and promotions to cater to individual user preferences or behavior. For example, you can display personalized greetings, recently viewed products, or location-based offers.

Segmentation: Divide your audience into smaller segments based on demographics, interests, or behavior patterns. This allows you to create targeted marketing campaigns and promotions that resonate with each segment.

23. Premiumization

👉 *The goal of premiumization is to create a perception of greater value in the minds of consumers, which can lead to increased demand and higher profit margins.*

Premiumization is the process of elevating a product or service to a higher perceived value in the eyes of consumers, often through higher prices, improved quality, or enhanced features.

Premiumization options

- Higher prices: One way to premiumize a product or service is to increase its price. This can create a perception of exclusivity and luxury, which can be appealing to some consumers.
- Improved quality: Another way to premiumize a product or service is to improve its quality. This can involve using higher-quality materials or ingredients, improving the manufacturing process, or adding features that enhance the user experience.
- Enhanced features: Adding new or enhanced features can also be a way to premiumize a product or service. This can include offering a wider range of options or customization, or providing additional services or benefits to customers.

Premiumization can be an effective strategy for increasing revenue and profit margins for businesses that are able to successfully create a perception of greater value in the minds of consumers.

However, it is important to carefully evaluate the market and target audience to ensure that premiumization is appropriate for the business and its customers.

Considerations for setting up premiumization

Identify your target audience and understand their preferences, needs, and willingness to pay for premium products or services.

Conduct market research to identify which products or services have the potential to be premiumized, and how much consumers are willing to pay for them.

Based on your target audience and market research, develop a premiumization strategy.

Communicate the value proposition of your premium products or services to your target audience, highlighting the unique features, benefits, and value that they offer.

Monitor the performance of your premium products or services and adjust your strategy as needed based on customer feedback and market trends.

Not all products are equally suitable for premiumization.

Products better suited for premiumization

Luxury or high-end products: Products that are already positioned as luxury or high-end, such as designer clothing or luxury watches, may be easier to premiumize because consumers already associate them with exclusivity and higher prices.

Unique or customized products: Products that are unique or customizable, such as personalized jewelry or custom-made furniture, may be easier to premiumize because consumers value the uniqueness and personalization that they offer.

High-quality or innovative products: Products that are of high quality or offer innovative features, such as high-tech electronics or eco-friendly products, may be easier to premiumize because consumers value the quality and performance that they offer.

Niche or specialized products: Products that are niche or specialized, such as artisanal foods or organic skincare products, may be easier to premiumize because consumers are willing to pay more for products that meet their specific needs or preferences.

Products with a strong brand identity: Products that have a strong brand identity, such as luxury cars or designer handbags, may be easier to premiumize because consumers associate the brand with exclusivity and high quality.

Example of premiumized products

Luxury is a core primiumization strategy used in all types of products including, apparel, beauty and cosmetics, automobiles, electronics, footwear, eyewear and more.

Services can also be premiumized including events, travel, and memberships.

24. Pricing strategy

👉 *An effective pricing strategy can help ecommerce businesses grow by attracting new customers, increase sales, and improve profitability.*

Pricing strategy for ecommerce refers to the methods and tactics used by ecommerce businesses to set prices for their products or services.

Common pricing strategies

Cost-plus pricing involves setting prices by adding a markup to the cost of producing or acquiring the product. This is a straightforward pricing method that ensures that the business covers its costs and makes a profit.

Value-based pricing involves setting prices based on the perceived value of the product or service to the customer. This method focuses on understanding customer needs and preferences and pricing accordingly.

Penetration pricing involves setting prices lower than the competition in order to gain market share and attract customers. This method is often used by new businesses entering a market or launching a new product.

Dynamic pricing involves setting prices based on real-time market conditions, such as supply and demand, competitor prices, and customer behavior. This method can help adjust prices in real-time to maximize profits without manual work.

Bundle pricing involves grouping products together and offering them at a discounted price compared to buying them separately. This method can increase sales by encouraging customers to purchase multiple products.

How pricing strategies impact conversion

Competitive pricing with respect to other retailers can help to create a sense of value and make customers more likely to choose your ecommerce site over others.

Pricing psychology such as using odd numbers, using discounts, or emphasizing the savings, can help to create a sense of urgency and encourage customers to make a purchase.

Tiered pricing tiers based on features or quantities can help to create a sense of value and encourage customers to purchase larger quantities or higher-priced items.

Displaying price comparisons with other retailers can help to build trust and confidence in the pricing of your products.

Displaying total cost of ownership pricing especially in combination with other competitors can highlight the overall cost to customers. This is highly used in electric car pricing where the tax and other monetary benefits are used to show reduced total costs.

25. Recommendations

☞ *Providing relevant recommendations throughout the customer journey can improve not only the likelihood of a sale, but also customer satisfaction and loyalty.*

Recommendations are an effective instrument for increasing customer satisfaction and boosting sales.

Recommendations are an important part of the ecommerce experience where customers have a lot of options. Product managers can help customers discover new products they might not have considered otherwise by providing relevant and personalized product recommendations.

The science of how recommendations are created by systems is a complex, behind the scenes, combination of data science, product data, information architecture and AI, both traditional machine-learning as well as new Generative AI technologies.

At the core a recommendations engine will consider the following to get to "know the customer" and make recommendations which make sense to them, one customer at a time:

- Shopping habits of the user, on-site and off if available,
- Favorites and dislikes
- Data and information in real time from various sources

The art of recommendations is what product managers and their teams collaborating with merchandisers, marketers and customer advocates bring together in where and when to introduce the best recommendations and "fine-tune" the software to the customer.

As mentioned in other topics, setting up a recommendation system for your website or app is not a once-and-done endeavor. If your company desires to optimize growth, this is yet another area where continuous monitoring, evaluation and improvement is needed.

We can not just rely on the software to get everything right. This is the human side of building growth engines, it takes time and attention, but we are fortunate to have ever more powerful software tools in our tool chest to help.

Example of impactful recommendations

Sephora is a good case study for recommendation, and one I'll be diving deeper into as part of the accompanying tool. The makeup and cosmetics use case is very interesting since it is so individualized and subjective and what works for one customer might not work for the others.

At Sephora, when a customer browses for a specific product personalized recommendations for other products that they might be interested in based on their browsing and purchase history.

For example, if a customer is looking for a moisturizer, Sephora may recommend other skincare products that they have purchased in the past or that are popular among customers with similar interests.

Amazon, eBay, Alibaba, and many other companies use product recommendations and this is often a key platform feature when selecting an ecommerce platform.

26. Reviews and Ratings

☛ *For ecommerce businesses, reviews can provide valuable feedback that can be used to improve products and services, as well as the overall customer experience. In addition reviews can help to build trust and credibility with potential customers, which can lead to sales growth and better customer loyalty.*

Reviews are feedback or comments provided by customers who have purchased and used a product or service from an ecommerce website.

These reviews can be submitted by customers on the ecommerce website, and are often used to provide information and feedback to other customers who are considering purchasing the same product.

Ecommerce reviews can be written in many different formats, including star ratings, written comments, photos, and videos and can provide valuable insights into the quality, performance, and usability of a product, as well as the customer service and overall experience provided by the ecommerce website.

Top companies/websites that use reviews to drive growth:

- Amazon's review system allows customers to provide detailed feedback on the products they've purchased through star ratings, comments, and media.
- Facebook allows users to create profiles, connect with others, and follow their favorite businesses or brands.
- Google Business Profile is a free tool for businesses to manage their online presence across Google, including Search and Maps.

Other top product review sites are, Yelp, TripAdvisor, Better Business Bureau (BBB), Angie's List, Foursquare, Glassdoor, Yellow Pages.

Challenges with reviews

Although there are many benefits to providing reviews on your ecommerce company and products, there are also some challenges to address.

Fake Reviews: one of the most significant challenges is the proliferation of fake reviews. Some individuals or competitors may post fraudulent positive or negative reviews to manipulate a product's reputation. This can mislead consumers and damage a business's credibility.

Review Bias: customers who have extremely positive or negative experiences are more likely to leave reviews. This bias can skew the overall rating of a product, as customers with moderate experiences may not be motivated to share their opinions.

Review Spam: businesses sometimes flood their product listings with fake or low-quality reviews to boost their ratings artificially. This not only misleads consumers but also undermines the trustworthiness of the review system.

Lack of Trust: due to the prevalence of fake reviews, some consumers have become skeptical of online reviews in general. This lack of trust can discourage potential buyers from relying on reviews when making purchasing decisions.

Limited Context: reviews often lack context, making it difficult for consumers to gauge whether a particular issue mentioned in a review is relevant to their needs. This can result in misinformed decisions.

Reviewer Anonymity: some review platforms allow users to post reviews anonymously or with pseudonyms. While anonymity can protect reviewers from retaliation, it can also make it harder to verify the authenticity of reviews.

Incentivized Reviews: some businesses offer incentives, such as discounts or free products, in exchange for positive reviews. This practice can lead to biased and less authentic feedback.

Inadequate Moderation: poorly moderated review platforms may struggle to filter out inappropriate or spammy content. This can create a negative user experience and harm the reputation of businesses using the platform.

Review Bombing: in some cases, organized groups or individuals may engage in review bombing, where they leave a large number of negative reviews on a product or business without valid reasons. This can harm a business's reputation unfairly.

Language and Cultural Differences: reviews may be written in different languages or by customers from diverse cultural backgrounds, which can lead to misunderstandings or misinterpretations.

Product Variation: some products have multiple variations (e.g., different colors, sizes) within the same product listing. Reviews for one variation may not apply to others, causing confusion for shoppers.

Review Manipulation by Businesses: some businesses may selectively highlight positive reviews and downplay or hide negative ones, which can mislead consumers looking for balanced feedback.

Unfortunately many of these challenges are ongoing so selecting the best partner to not only provide the software but also continue monitoring and mitigation is good.

How to select a reviews management vendor

Important points to consider when selecting a review solution provider or software:

Review Collection: the ability to collect and display customer reviews is the core function of review software. Look for software that provides an easy and convenient way for customers to submit reviews including star ratings, written reviews, and even photo or video submissions.

Integration with Your Ecommerce Platform: seamless integration with your ecommerce platform is crucial for efficient data exchange ensuring customer reviews are automatically displayed on your product pages, improving the overall shopping experience.

Moderation Tools: moderation tools are essential for maintaining the quality of reviews on your website. You should be able to filter out spam, offensive content, or irrelevant reviews.

Rich Snippets for SEO Benefits: rich snippets are structured data markup that provides search engines with additional information about your content. When review software generates rich snippets, your product pages may appear with star ratings, review counts, and other information in search engine results.

Email and Post-Purchase Review Request Capabilities: to encourage customers to leave reviews, your review software should offer email and post-purchase review request capabilities. Automated email reminders can prompt customers to share their feedback after they've made a purchase.

Social Sharing Options: social sharing options allow customers to easily share their reviews on social media platforms.

Analytics and Reporting: analytics and reporting tools provide insights into the performance of your review section. You should be able to track metrics like review submission rates, average ratings, and the impact of reviews on conversions.

Customization Options for Review Display: customization features allow you to tailor the appearance of review widgets and the way reviews are displayed on your website. This ensures that the review section aligns with your brand's design and aesthetics. Look for options to change colors, fonts, layouts, and widget placement.

Ongoing monitoring and support: review fraud is an ongoing problem for companies and if it's not being monitored regularly it will become a major issue. Your software provider should help with ongoing support, either directly or in conjunction with their own partner network.

27. Returns

👉 *Returns directly impact the most important metrics and drag down growth. As growth product managers we want to understand what the reason for our returns are and work on ways to reduce it.*

The return problem in ecommerce is a significant challenge, and it's likely to remain a significant issue in the e-commerce industry.

People return items purchased online for a variety of reasons, and the specific reasons can vary depending on the product category and individual preferences.

Why we return items

Some of the more common reasons for returning items purchased online include:

Size and Fit Issues: Clothing, shoes, and accessories are frequently returned because they don't fit properly or look as expected. Sizing discrepancies between brands can be a significant factor.

Quality and Defects: Customers may return items that arrive damaged, defective, or not as described. This applies to electronics, appliances, furniture, and other products.

Changed Mind: Sometimes, customers simply change their minds after receiving a product. This might be due to buyer's remorse or because the item doesn't meet their expectations in person.

Color and Appearance: Products may look different in online photos or on a computer screen compared to real life. This can lead to returns when the color or appearance doesn't match the customer's expectations.

Product categories with the highest returns

Not all products have the same return rates and characteristics. Product categories with the highest online returns include:

Fashion and Apparel: Clothing, shoes, and accessories often have high return rates. Customers may order multiple sizes or styles, try them on at home, and return items that don't fit or meet their expectations. Fit issues and variations in sizing between brands contribute to higher return rates in this category.

Electronics: Electronics, such as smartphones, laptops, and cameras, can also have a significant return rate. Reasons for returns include product defects, compatibility issues, and buyer's remorse. Additionally, some customers may use electronics temporarily for specific needs and then return them.

Home Decor and Furniture: Items like furniture, rugs, and home decor are often returned due to size, color, or style mismatches with customers' expectations. Returns in this category can be costly due to shipping and handling.

Cosmetics and Personal Care Products: Personal care and beauty products can have high return rates due to factors like allergies, skin sensitivities, or simply not meeting customers' expectations regarding color or effectiveness.

Jewelry: Jewelry returns are not uncommon, often due to differences in perceived quality or the item not matching the recipient's taste or style.

Strategies to reduce returns

Reducing returns is important for improving profitability, customer satisfaction, and operational efficiency. Here are some strategies ecommerce businesses can use to reduce returns:

Improve product descriptions and visuals: Providing accurate and detailed product descriptions and high-quality visuals can help customers make informed purchasing decisions, reducing the likelihood of returns due to product dissatisfaction.

Offer virtual try-on and fitting tools: Providing virtual try-on and fitting tools can help customers choose the right size and fit for clothing and accessories, reducing the likelihood of returns due to sizing issues.

Provide customer reviews and ratings: Customer reviews and ratings can provide valuable feedback to other customers, helping them make more informed purchasing decisions and reducing the likelihood of returns due to product dissatisfaction.

Streamline the return process: Making the return process easy and hassle-free can encourage customers to make purchases with confidence, knowing that they can easily return products if necessary.

Use data analytics to identify trends and issues: Using data analytics to analyze returns data can help ecommerce businesses identify trends and issues, such as products that have high return rates or specific reasons for returns, allowing them to take corrective action.

Improve product quality and consistency: Improving product quality and consistency can reduce the likelihood of returns due to product defects or inconsistencies.

Handling returns

Handling returns can be a complex and time-consuming process, but there are a number of tools and technologies available to help ecommerce businesses streamline the process and improve customer satisfaction. Some examples include:

Return management software: There are a range of return management software tools available that can help ecommerce businesses automate the returns process, including software that generates return labels, tracks returns, and processes refunds.

Customer service tools: use customer service tools such as live chat or chatbots to provide customers with real-time support and assistance with the returns process.

Analytics tools: Analytics tools can help track return rates, identify trends, and pinpoint areas where improvements can be made.

Packaging and shipping tools: use packaging and shipping tools to ensure that returns are processed efficiently and securely, such as tools that provide tracking information or offer prepaid return shipping labels.

Employee training: train employees on how to handle returns, including how to communicate with customers and how to process refunds.

28. Rental

👉 *As product leaders offering a rental model for your products can be a lucrative business for your products if the products are conducive to rental as well as a customer profile willing to try and rent your items.*

A rental retail company, also known as a rental store or rental service, is a type of business that offers customers the opportunity to temporarily use or borrow items in exchange for a fee.

Rental can be the core business or it can be a supplement to a classic ecommerce transactional business model, or you can partner with rental companies to get rid of your unsold items and usable returns more efficiently.

The rental business model aligns with the sharing economy and sustainability concepts. It offers a way for individuals to experience luxury fashion without the need for permanent ownership, reducing waste associated with the fashion industry's fast turnover.

Rental retail companies can provide a cost-effective and convenient solution for individuals and businesses that require items temporarily without the need for long-term ownership. This business model can also contribute to resource sharing, reducing waste and environmental impact by promoting the reuse of items.

These companies provide a wide range of products for rent, catering to various consumer needs and preferences.

The items available for rent can include:

Consumer Goods: This category includes everyday items that people might need temporarily, such as tools, appliances, electronics, furniture, and recreational equipment like bicycles, camping gear, and sporting equipment.

Specialty Items: Some rental retail companies specialize in providing unique or infrequently used items, such as party supplies, event equipment, costumes, audio-visual equipment, and event space.

Vehicles: Many rental retail companies offer cars, trucks, vans, and other types of vehicles for short-term use, often catering to travelers, individuals needing temporary transportation, or businesses needing delivery or moving services.

Construction and Industrial Equipment: Some rental retail companies focus on providing heavy machinery, construction equipment, and industrial tools to contractors and businesses that may not need these items on a permanent basis.

Home Improvement Equipment: These companies offer tools and equipment for DIY projects, renovations, and repairs, allowing customers to access specialized tools without purchasing them.

Home and Garden Equipment: Lawnmowers, leaf blowers, pressure washers, and other garden tools can be rented from these companies, especially useful for seasonal or occasional tasks.

The rental process typically involves customers paying a fee based on the duration of the rental period. This fee can vary depending on the type of item being rented and the rental duration. Some rental companies also offer additional services, such as delivery, setup, and maintenance of the rented items.

Rent the Runway is a famous rental business specializing in renting designer clothing, dresses, and accessories for special occasions or everyday wear. Customers can select items online, rent them for a specific period, and return them after use.

Benefits of rental ecommerce businesses

A rental e-commerce business offers several unique benefits that can differentiate it from traditional retail models.

Cost Savings for Customers: customers can access and use products without the high upfront costs associated with purchasing.

Variety and Experimentation: access to a wide variety of products that customers might not normally purchase due to cost or infrequent use.

Environmental Sustainability: promotes sharing and reuse, contributing to environmental sustainability.

Storage Space Savings: Many items, like sports equipment or tools, can take up a significant amount of storage space. A rental model eliminates the need for customers to store these items when not in use.

Access to Premium and High-End Products: rental platforms often offer high-quality and premium products that might be financially out of reach for many customers to purchase outright.

Convenience: offer the convenience of online shopping and doorstep delivery. Customers can browse, select, and order items from the comfort of their homes, saving time and effort.

Reduced Depreciation: For products that tend to depreciate quickly in value, such as electronics or certain fashion items, renting eliminates the concern about value loss over time.

29. Resale and re-commerce

👉 *Offering a resale program can improve growth by providing a way for customers to recoup some of the cost of products they purchase from you and additional upsell and cross-sell opportunities among other benefits.*

Resale refers to the act of selling previously owned or used goods. Resale takes place in physical stores as well as online in today's world and can include a range of products, including clothing, electronics, home goods, and more.

Consumers are looking for ways to reduce waste and save money so there is a strong pull demand from the consumer side for pre-owned and resale items.

Options for engaging in resale

Online marketplaces such as eBay, Poshmark, and thredUP allow individuals to buy and sell secondhand goods, creating a more sustainable and affordable alternative to traditional retail.

In addition to general marketplaces, some ecommerce businesses have also started to incorporate resale into their business models to take advantage of the brand value and interest consumers have in their products.

For example, some fashion retailers now offer a resale platform on their website, allowing customers to buy and sell pre-owned clothing items.

Is resale a good option for your products?

To determine if it is a good idea to set up a resale site for your brand consider your brand values, target audience, and business objectives.

- Brand values: If your brand values sustainability and social responsibility, setting up resale could align with your brand values and help promote a more sustainable and ethical business model.
- Target audience: If your target audience is interested in sustainability and affordability, setting up resale could help

attract and retain customers who are looking for more
sustainable and affordable shopping options.

- Business objectives: If your business objectives include
  increasing revenue and profitability, setting up resale could help
  generate additional revenue from secondhand sales.
- Brand perception: Setting up resale can affect the perceived
  value and exclusivity of your brand.

Resale can help growth by attracting new customers and generating
additional revenue.

A resale program can also attract new customers who are looking for
sustainable and affordable shopping options and generate additional
revenue.

30. Retention

👉 *Increasing retention (minimizing churn) contributes to growth by keeping a larger number of customers active and making repeat purchases. Low retention (high churn) drag growth down, reduce margins and lower the LTV.*

Retention is the practice of keeping a customer engaged with the company and products so they will continue purchasing from us.

The counter to retention is called churn, which is when we lose a customer. Churn is bad because acquiring new customers is expensive and we always want to create long term relationships with our customers so they buy from us again.

Retention is tracked and measured mainly using what is called the churn rate which is the percentage of customers who have discontinued their engagement with the business within a given time frame.

The process and journey a customer takes to go into the churn zone for your business is where product managers can understand granularly and devise specific actions and playbooks to address and minimize churn.

For units-sole retail companies churn can take longer to understand and address while for subscription product companies it can be quicker (stopping or not renewing subscriptions).

To calculate churn rate, you can use the following formula:

Churn Rate = (Number of Customers Lost during a Period / Total Number of Customers at the Beginning of the Period) x 100

Detecting churn and improving retention

Before we dive deeper into details let's set our expectations on what our specific churn rate should be so we have something to work towards.

Churn rates can differ significantly between industries and types of ecommerce businesses.

For example, subscription-based businesses might have different churn expectations compared to one-time purchase stores, rental and marketplaces.

Levels of churn can also depend on the stage of business growth, market competition, and the quality of customer experience.

To determine an acceptable churn rate for your ecommerce business, consider factors such as:

- Your business goals
- Financial projections,
- Customer acquisition costs,
- Customer lifetime value, and
- Industry benchmarks or trends

Regularly monitor your churn rate, analyze trends, and compare them to industry averages to gauge how well you're retaining customers and where improvements can be made.

Product Manager's role in retention

As product managers our work on retention is two-fold,

- Detect when churn is happening or about to happen
- Take measures to minimize it.

Each of these steps is equally important and not useful without the other.

Churn signals are key changes in customer behavior which can tell us about when they are a potential churn candidate. Some of the common churn signals include noticeable drops in the frequency of purchases, declines in customer's average order value (AOV) decreases over time, decreased activity with website or app, increasing number of abandoned carts, unopened emails and expired credit cards.

There are of course more direct indications including customer complaints to customer service and negative social media comments.

There are also seasonal factors in purchase behaviors around your specific products and also personal life events and other societal events outside our control.

Churn is a fact of life for companies and our goal is to first understand it and then take action to reduce it continually.

Having the tools that automate churn detection is key to having a robust predictive intelligence process which is not manual. Companies such as Qualtrics have powerful customer analytics however it's important to dive deep into specifically what specific capabilities does any tool provide to detect churn.

Retention tools and automation

What I personally look for in a tool's churn detection capability is providing automatic (preferably real time) customer level behavior and patterns over different time frames including a churn score to track over time. On top of that automated notifications as well as self service controls for enacting some predefined attributes such as price and bundling.

When churn has been detected we need to take actions to minimize it.

Actions such as reducing product quality, improved experience, personalization and communication, offers and easier returns and refunds, over-delivering on expectations are some activities which will help minimize churn.

In addition features such as loyalty programs, branded credit cards, vibrant communities and outstanding customer service are effective in creating a more loyal customer base.

Churn programs cost money and take time and resources so cost is also important in devising churn reduction programs. Ultimately you don't want churn activities costing more than customer acquisition. If the company has high margins or high LTV potential more investment in churn is often justifiable.

31. Search

☞ *An optimized search functionality on ecommerce sites can increase conversion and growth by 40% or more according to some studies. This number can be different between product categories but it is very significant.*

Search is a core functionality for ecommerce, without which customers can not find products they are looking for.

Search is provided in two main formats:

- Text based search typically in a text field where the results can be present to customers.
- Faceted search which is in terms of categories, price, color, size and other filters conveniently found by customers.

Search is important for ecommerce websites because it allows customers to quickly find what they are looking for, reducing the amount of time and effort required to navigate through a website.

Displaying search results

Displaying search results is the most important benefit of the search function so care has to be taken to provide an easy to understand results experience, as well as robust performance to provide the results quickly.

In addition accuracy and relevance are key in providing a great search experience to customers. Inaccurate or unrelated results will only frustrate users and can lead to early exits from the site.

Measuring the performance of search functionality is important in determining if and how to improve the experience for users.

Search Results Click-Through Rate (CTR) is a key metric used to measure the performance of your search features.

Another useful metric is the search refinement rate which tells us the percentage of searches that are refined or modified by customers after their initial search query. A high overall refinement rate can indicate the initial results are not highly useful and customers have to keep trying to find the products they are looking for.

Search abandonment rate is also important to measure to understand what percentage of users do not engage with search results.

Implementing search for ecommerce

Modern ecommerce platforms normally come with embedded search functionality. However, the out-of-the-box search functionality has limited utility for large ecommerce operations with multiple product categories, large and changing catalogs and high transaction volumes.

For larger ecommerce companies there are special search tools such as Solr and Algolia.

Searchandising

Searchandising combines "search" and "merchandising" to optimize search results and the overall search experience.

Searchandising includes strategies to ensure that when a user searches for a product or a keyword, the search results not only match the query but also promote certain products or content based on merchandising priorities.

Key components of searchandising include Search Relevance, Merchandising Rules, Personalization, Promotions and Special Offers and Visual Merchandising.

Future of search

Search is such an important part of the customer experience, it actually starts from the initial search on search engines and extends to websites, or in a marketplace.

The overarching search experience is poised for significant disruption due to AI and other forms of human-machine interaction.

Some of the ways search is expected to evolve include Generative and Generalized AI agents, voice search, conversational interfaces and interaction, visual search, context awareness, Augmented Reality (AR) and VR, visual discovery and highly-individualized (1:1) personalization.

As product managers we need to stay informed of improvements in search and build experiments to learn how new forms of search might help our customers and provide better results for us.

32. Shipping and Delivery

☛ *Shipping and delivery options are one of the key factors in consumer decisions on the buy question. Lack of or un-interesting shipping options will impact growth negatively.*

How and when customers receive your products can play a key difference and competitive advantage for your ecommerce and retail business.

There are multiple tools in the fulfillment tool chest you can utilize and experiment with and in all cases you can expect a positive impact on your key metrics, if the tool is a fit for your products and customers.

The process of managing getting products purchased to them is called fulfillment.

Common fulfillment options

There are many options for managing your fulfillment including:

Self-Fulfillment where you manage all aspects of order fulfillment, including storing inventory, picking, packing, and shipping. This is best for large scale retail operations and not a good fit for small ecommerce companies.

Use Third-Party Logistics (3PL) companies who handle various aspects of fulfillment, from inventory storage to shipping.

Use dropshipping so you don't need to hold inventory and pass customer orders to your suppliers who then ship products directly to your customers.

Multi-Channel Fulfillment: involves using multiple channels (physical stores, online marketplaces, etc.) to fulfill orders. Inventory is often shared between channels to optimize efficiency.

Ship-from-Store: retail stores are used as fulfillment centers, allowing customers to receive items from their local store, speeding up delivery, and better for the environment.

Crowdshipping: utilizing local couriers to deliver packages, especially for 1-hour (or faster), same-day or last-mile delivery.

Fulfilled by Amazon (FBA) by sending inventory to Amazon's warehouses, and having Amazon handle storage, packing, shipping, and customer service.

Pick-Up Lockers are secure storage units installed at physical locations such as retail stores, shopping centers, transit stations, or other convenient spots.

Drones and delivery robots are also in development and likely be more common forms of getting products to customers at the local, last mile level.

We can also utilize specific discounting and special offers in providing different fulfillment options to improve business metrics specially conversion rates, revenues and Lifetime value.

Free Shipping

Free or discounted shipping is a highly effective growth technique used by online stores to provide customers with the benefit of not paying additional fees while placing orders for specific items.

For example, Amazon provides free delivery to its Amazon Prime members for eligible orders, while Sephora offers free delivery on orders exceeding a specific amount and two-day shipping for Sephora Flash members.

Customers are more inclined to buy products when they know that they can avail free delivery, and it may also encourage them to come back for future purchases. Furthermore, free delivery can help distinguish a business from its competitors and enhance customer satisfaction.

Zappos (purchased by Amazon) attributes a large part of its success to its free delivery policy, which has helped to increase customer loyalty and drive sales growth.

BOPIS (Buy Online Pick Up In Store)

"BOPIS" stands for "Buy Online, Pick Up In Store" and allows customers to place orders for products online through a retailer's website or app and then pick up their purchases at a physical store location.

BOPIS combines the convenience of online shopping with the immediacy of in-store pickup, and picked up in popularity significantly during the Covid Pandemic and is here to stay.

Last mile delivery

Getting products in customers' hands is the last part of the shipping process ecommerce companies manage. Depending on the type of product and location of inventory there are different options for the final delivery.

For example fresh food items must be delivered quickly using humans or with newer methods being developed such as robots and drones.

Apparel and manufactured items can be shipped across continents and delivered to customers either with US postal service, UPS or Amazon delivery as some of the most common options.

Delivery time

Shipping and delivery time is also a factor in customer decisions and experience with the company. With quicker delivery options offered by Amazon retailers and ecommerce companies are regularly being compared to Amazon delivery when offering estimated times to customers.

If the same item is available on Amazon with same or next day delivery customers will purchase on amazon rather than waiting longer.

Return shipping

Return shipping is also a factor as it can take time to ship the items to the company, wait for processing and wait to receive replacement items. Clear and regular communication is very effective in providing customers with peace of mind that your company cares about their experience.

33. SMS and Messaging commerce

☛ *SMS has a much higher open ratio and if utilized effectively can result in growing sales while providing a unique shopping experience for customers. SMS can also be used effectively for transactional and engagement communication with positive contribution to growth.*

SMS shopping or text shopping as it's also known as is a form of shopping where customers interact with retailers, personal shoppers, or customer service representatives through text messages (SMS) to make purchases, inquire about products, or receive personalized recommendations.

Best practices for using SMS

Consider the following best practices and potential challenges when using SMS:

Make sure customers have opted in to receive SMS messages from your company.

Be mindful of the frequency of your messages. Too many messages can be perceived as spam.

Send messages at appropriate times to avoid disrupting customers.

Adhere to privacy and data protection regulations, such as GDPR.

Clearly communicate the purpose of your SMS and include a call-to-action.

Examples of SMS commerce

Utilizing SMS in ecommerce can take a few forms:

- Pure SMS apps such as Magic and Alfred. They have had mixed results however this was many years ago so the conditions have changed.
- Add SMS as a sales method to our ecommerce website or app. For example Walmart Text-to-shop engages customers by chatting along the discovery and search journey.

- Using SMS for post-order updates including shipping progress and delivery confirmation is a useful and often acceptable use for consumers.

Grocery and food is a good use case for SMS

Text Message
Today 10:16 AM

Sprouts: Buy One, Get One 50% off on fresh produce, deli favorites and more 12/6-12/12! https://sfm.us/KY8zc/J6

An added benefit of SMS is that with customers which also have smart watches like Apple Watch the notifications go to the phone as well.

Messaging apps

Depending on your customer segment, and geographical reach using messaging apps is also an effective channel. Messaging apps including WhatsApp, Facebook messenger, Instagram and Snapchat can be effective to help shoppers buy in their preferred channels.

Here's an example of a WhatsApp shop in India. WhatsApp shopping is a lot more prevalent outside the US. Meta, owner of WhatsApp, is making a push to build the adoption globally.

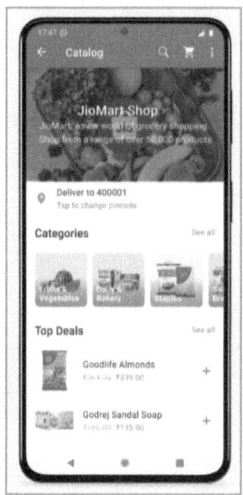

Build Vs. Buy

In both SMS and messaging cases companies can build the capabilities internally or buy outsourced solutions. Companies including Twilio, Attentive are good starting points to investigate options for SMS and there are consulting agencies to help setup messaging shops.

34. Social Commerce

☛ *Social commerce contributes to growth by letting consumers purchase produce directly from where they are introduced to them, on social channels and apps.*

Social commerce is a subset of e-commerce that involves the use of social media platforms to market and sell products and services. It allows consumers to discover, research, and purchase products directly within social media apps, without having to leave the platform.

Social commerce has become increasingly popular in recent years, as more and more people spend time on social media. In 2022, global social commerce sales reached $560 billion, and are expected to reach $1.8 trillion by 2027.

There are a number of benefits to social commerce for both businesses and consumers. For businesses, social commerce provides a way to reach a large and engaged audience with their products and services. It also allows businesses to build relationships with customers and create a more personalized shopping experience.

Consumers can discover new products, compare prices, and make purchases all in one place. Social commerce also allows consumers to get recommendations from friends and family, and to read reviews from other customers.

As ecommerce product managers looking for opportunities to grow our product's reach and revenues it's prudent for us to investigate, be informed or experiment with using social commerce. Implementing a full plan involves different teams in the org including engineering, marketing and finance. The goal should be to find ways to run small experiments to capture data before making a full commitment.

Here are some options for experimenting and implementing social commerce:

Facebook Shops: Brands can set up free Facebook Shops within their Facebook business profile.

Facebook Live Shopping: Introduced in 2021, Live Shopping Fridays lets Facebook users see products in action, ask questions and make purchases all in real time.

Instagram shoppable posts: Instagram's shoppable posts are linked to a Facebook Shop account. Brands with a lot of visual content can make great use of Instagram's layout and Stories to link to in-app product pages.

Pinterest product Pins: Pinterest's product Pins are expected to account for 15.7% of all US social buyers by 2023. Unlike typical pins, product Pins provide space for price and availability details and redirect to product landing pages.

Sephora is a French beauty retailer that has been a pioneer in social commerce. The company was one of the first to experiment with live shopping and influencer marketing. Sephora also has a robust social media presence, with over 20 million followers on Instagram. The company uses social media to share beauty tips, tutorials, and product recommendations.

There are many more large and small retail companies engaging and experimenting with social commerce and it's good to keep an eye on this growth option for your product.

Keep in mind to set success metrics and select measurable metrics to gauge your success. As we've learned from experience so far, likes and comments alone are not the best measures of success in social commerce.

35. Styling and personal shopping

☛*For ecommerce businesses, styling and personal shopping can help growth by providing increased sales conversion, enhanced customer loyalty, improved customer satisfaction and other benefits.*

Ecommerce styling services refer to a type of service offered by some ecommerce websites that helps customers choose and purchase clothing and accessories based on their personal style preferences.

These services can range from simple product recommendations to more personalized styling assistance, with the goal of providing a higher level of service and improving the customer experience.

Benefits of styling and personal shopping

There are multiple benefits for offering styling and personal shopping for all involved.

For shoppers they get access to additional services to a well-styled and curated wardrobe which can create a positive first impression in personal and professional settings.

Shoppers also can save time by eliminating the need to browse through numerous stores and online platforms. This is a key value proposition for higher income and busy consumers.

Stylists can also help individuals build a versatile wardrobe with mix-and-match options, ensuring that they make the most of their clothing as well as learn about different and newer styles and brands most consumers may not know about.

Businesses offering personal shopping services can experience increased sales as customers are guided toward products that suit their preferences.

The high touch nature of personal shopping and styling also fosters a stronger connection between customers and brands, leading to increased brand loyalty and help the retailer be better differentiated in the market.

Personal shoppers can specifically improve cross-selling and upselling opportunities leading to increased revenues and other improved KPIs.

There are also additional societal benefits by creating new jobs in the form of stylists, fashion consultants, personal shoppers and retail personnel.

Stylists and expert personal shoppers can guide individuals toward making more sustainable fashion choices, contributing to the growing awareness of environmental and ethical concerns in the fashion industry.

Styling services options and planning

Virtual styling assistance where customers can chat with a stylist or receive personalized recommendations based on their style preferences and other factors.

Personal shopping services where customers can receive one-on-one assistance from a stylist or personal shopper to help them choose clothing and accessories that fit their style and budget.

With subscription styling services customers receive a regular delivery of curated clothing and accessories based on their style preferences and history.

Personal styling services can contribute to growth by enhancing the customer experience leading to increased Engagement, higher conversion rates and reducing returns.

There is also a level of differentiation and potential PR you can gain by offering a styling service, specially in the super crowded retail industry.

Consumers are also apt to be more loyal to brands and retailers which care to invest in personally helping them with styling services.

Implementation and offering a styling program requires careful consideration and planning and can include the build vs buy decision.

Hiring and training skilled stylists, setting up communication channels, and managing the additional workload are time consuming and can be costly to set up and maintain.

There are also technical parts of the offering including video chat, appointment booking and ecommerce integration which will make a complete experience.

Outsourcing your styling offering

Partnering with third-party stylists or styling services can be a strategic approach to offering personal styling services without the need to build an in-house team from scratch.

This approach can save you time and resources while still providing your customers with the personalized experience they desire.

There are many local stylists which can help you to get started although the cost might be high as they charge per hour. You can also use national services that are being created at lower costs and can be implemented in different cities if you have a national or regional footprint.

Examples of styling services

Some famous retailers offering online and in-person styling services include Anthropologie, Neiman Marcus and Nordstrom. As you can see this is a service best suited for higher prices and consideration items.

Potential challenges

One of the main challenges, and shortcomings, of online styling offerings is the lack of integration with the ecommerce applications to complete the purchase right in the session. This gap adds a friction point which can lead to lost sales and not a good experience for consumers.

Another challenge I have seen is the stylists are in their homes and just reviewing what the customer can already find on the brand's website to them.

While the idea can be somewhat useful it falls short of the real retail experience where the stylist can actually be in a store and take the shopper on a discovery experience. Of course providing a robust in-store virtual styling experience involves much more than just the technology.

Many companies have learned, the hard way, that we can not rely on store staff to do customer sessions since their main responsibility is taking care of the store and customers who are there in person.

It is a positive sign that companies are experimenting with extending their service level to online shoppers and as an ecommerce or omni-channel retailer, if your product mix and customer base is a fit I recommend trying the styling service.

36. Stores

👉 *Physical proximity to customers including different types of stores, provides growth levers not possible with pure play ecommerce.*

This may sound blasphemous to pure ecommerce pros, but it's being proven over and over again that having physical stores actually adds to an ecommerce operations reach and growth.

Even before the COVID-19 pandemic the ecommerce industry was waking up to the fact that:

Pure Play ecommerce companies are hitting a (virtual wall) in how much market share they can capture, within all the variations of customer experiences and expectations.

As long as we are selling to humans, which are highly social and sensory beings, there are just some aspects of the shopping experience which are not available with ecommerce, even the most advanced and far our futuristic formats and experiences do not, always, in every case meet consumer needs.

And some aspects of the ecommerce business including the vaunted customer acquisition cost (CAC) are becoming prohibitively expensive and consumer attention is increasingly difficult to get online.

What we've learned is that the physical store and proximity to consumers actually adds to ecommerce, even if you don't carry inventory in the location, it is a different and unique experience with a much higher chance of connecting with consumers.

Physical presence options

There are a few options for ecommerce companies to get into the physical retail space:

Retail stores which are full fledged retail stores with inventory and sales to customers

Guideshops which are retail locations purely for information and carry no inventory.

Pop up shops are short term retail stores with inventory and sales.

Retail stores can provide several benefits for ecommerce businesses, even though they primarily operate online. Benefits include brand visibility and awareness, instilling trust and credibility, seeing customers interaction with products, instant gratification, returns and exchanges, local SEO and foot traffic and networking, events and partnerships.

Having multiple channels including stores also adds diversification and risk mitigation in case one of the channels becomes challenged by internal or external events.

Pop up shops

Pop-up shops, also known as temporary retail or pop-up stores, are short-term, temporary retail spaces that allow businesses to set up a physical presence for a limited period of time, often ranging from a few days to several months.

These shops "pop up" in a location and then disappear after the designated time frame, which can create a sense of urgency and excitement for customers.

Pop-up shops are becoming more common and provide a flexible and creative way for brands to engage with customers, test new markets, launch products, and create unique shopping experiences.

Pop-Up Shop benefits include limited duration, location variety, creative themes and fast and less expensive ways for testing and expansion before committing to a permanent location.

Many shopping centers and retail landlords are more favorable to pop-up shops and even have pre-designed programs for these.

Retail distribution

Of course, the oldest form of retail is the distribution model where you can have your products sold in department stores, boutiques and other retail stores.

This model is actually becoming more popular with pure Direct-to-Consumer brands as well.

Many large brands are utilizing the multi-channel strategy including:

- Brand owned retail stores
- Brand owned online commerce
- Retail distribution
- Online marketplaces

A good example of this is Lululemon, the athletic wear company which has its own stores, an online ecommerce website, selling through retailers such as Nordstrom.

37. Subscriptions

☛ *For businesses, subscriptions can provide predictable revenue, improved customer retention and loyalty, and upselling and cross-selling opportunities leading to growth.*

A subscription is a business model in which customers pay a recurring fee, typically on a monthly, quarterly, or yearly basis, to access a product or service.

Subscriptions can be used in various industries, including media, software, entertainment, and ecommerce.

In ecommerce subscriptions can provide several benefits for both customers including convenience, cost savings, and a sense of value and exclusivity. For the business they provide recurring revenue and a level of predictability not available with pure product sale models.

More enhanced subscription programs allow the customer to set the renewal at what works for them, not what the company decides. This requires additional work on the back end for the company but is a good example of customer centricity.

Examples of subscription commerce

The subscription model can be applied in different product categories including fashion, food, eyewear and more.

Fashion companies such as Stitch Fix and Frank and Oak are examples of pure subscription models which provide a monthly curated selection of clothing and accessories based on their style preferences. Customers can keep one or all of the products or return them for other options.

Food delivery companies also are heavily investing in subscription options which can be specially profitable due to the higher frequency of food consumption.

Types of subscription models

Subscription models range from pure subscriptions to hybrid models where the subscription is combined with one or more other revenue models.

- Pure subscription, where the company only offers this type of purchase option to customers. Stitch Fix is a popular example of the pure subscription model. Men's shaving products such as Dollar Shave Club is also another successful example.
- Product sales plus subscription, where the main format is product sales and the company also offers subscription orders. One example of this model is the Amazon Subscribe and Save.
- Subscription plus rental, where customers can subscribe to a rental model. A successful example of this model is Nuuly (by Urban Outfitters) where Each subscription allows renters to borrow six items at a time for $88 a month.

Customers typically expect to receive some form of discount from unit product sales when ordering on a subscription.

Popular subscription product categories

Subscriptions are especially popular for food and consumable products and apparel primarily because consumers know they need these products regularly and don't want to spend the time to repeatedly order them.

- Meal Kit Delivery companies deliver pre-portioned ingredients and recipes to subscribers.
- Beauty and Personal Care products including beauty, shaving and grooming.
- Fitness and Wellness including fitness classes, supplements and health products.
- Book and Audiobook Service including Monthly book subscriptions and audiobooks.

- Subscription Boxes which are Curated boxes with various themes and Niche products (pet food, gaming, etc.).
- Clothing and Fashion subscriptions including rental and luxury designer items.
- Coffee and Tea Subscriptions to deliver specialty coffee or tea to subscribers weekly or monthly.

Designing a subscription business

When considering a subscription business model we need to think through several factors:

Clearly define the target market for your subscription service. Understand their needs, preferences, and pain points. Selecting a niche can improve odds of success considerably.

Clearly articulate the unique value your subscription provides. What problem does it solve for your customers and why should they subscribe?

Choose the type of subscription model that best fits your business and customer base. Common models were listed in the previous section.

Determine your pricing strategy including factors such as the perceived value of your offering, competitor pricing, and the willingness of your target audience to pay.

Consider encouraging potential subscribers by offering trial periods, free samples, or limited-time promotions.

Provide personalized experiences by allowing subscribers to customize their subscriptions based on.

Plan and invest in a robust engagement and retention program.

38. Video

☞ *A picture is worth a thousand words, and by extension a video can be more valuable than static photos for customers in deciding what to purchase. Video improves conversion and growth by providing an enhanced level of Visual Engagement by allowing potential customers to see the product from different angles, in various lighting conditions, and in action.*

Video, in recorded or live forms have been gaining attraction for consumers and not just in watching funny cat videos but also in shopping.

Recorded video

Research has shown that consumers are more likely to make a purchase after watching a video. For instance, a report by Wyzowl found that 84% of consumers have been convinced to buy a product or service after watching a brand's video.

Demonstration of features and benefits can remove doubt and questions for making a purchase. Seeing a product in action through videos can create a more realistic and authentic representation. This helps in building trust with customers as they can get a better sense of what to expect from the actual product, reducing the chances of disappointment upon receipt.

We can also use video to effectively and quickly tell a story about the product or the designer and creator. Through testimonials, demonstrations, or narrative storytelling, we can create an emotional connection with the customer. Emotional connections often drive purchasing decisions.

Video can also result in reduced return rates. When customers have a clear understanding of what they are purchasing, including its size, functionality, and appearance, there is less likelihood of dissatisfaction and return.

Shoppable video

Another form of recorded video used in shopping is what's called shoppable video. This is where items in a video are tagged by software so users can click or tap on them as the video is playing and be able to purchase them.

Retailers such as ASOS and Swarovski have used shoppable videos with success.

Live video

Another, newer aspect of using video for commerce is livestream (aka live) video.

Live video can be provided in different formats including public or private and has proven very effective in markets such as China. In the West live video has not yet caught on with consumers as it has in China but the trends are up and it is believed that the habit will take root with consumers although it may take longer.

Due to immature expectations on how live video would be received by consumers in the US there has been disappointment with many industry analysts of its effectiveness in the West.

As we well know, wrong expectations can ruin even the best of opportunities. Recently a more educated and nuanced set of expectations are being practiced and companies are conducting more mature experiments with better results.

There are still ways to go to match the adoption in China but we have a better chance of success with reset expectations.

There are two forms to live shopping experiences, public and private.

Public live shopping videos are of the 1-many format where one (or a team) of presenters are showing products in the livestream and multiple viewers are watching, and hopefully purchasing the products. Public livestreams can go from a person starting one by themselves in the home all the way to full professional productions conducted by major retailers such as Nordstrom and Walmart.

Literally all major social platforms in the West are experimenting with live shopping, specifically the public form, including Instagram, TikTok, Facebook, X (formerly Twitter) and even Amazon.

There is also the private live shopping experience which is limited to one or a small group of participants. Private live shopping is much more personalized and high tough and typically well suited for considered purchases, items that are more unique, cost more and require more research, consideration and ultimately help for the shoppers.

As we have seen with live shopping experimentation will need to continue and changes in strategy and tactics will be needed for each retailer to find the best mix.

Today the question is not If, but When live video will become a mass consumer shopping experience in the West.

As product managers we need to be informed and explore options to run limited experiments to capture data on how live video can benefit our customers. Live video experiments need to be tightly coordinated with marketing and in fact they are mainly driven by marketing and supported by product to implement and maintain.

There are a multitude of companies providing livestream shopping solutions and the industry is also tilting heavier on the use of influencers to pull the concept deeper into the masses.

When considering live shopping platforms pay attention to the overall User experience, integration capabilities, social interaction features such as chat, security of customer data.

Many platforms offer a trial period so take advantage of this to assess the platform's suitability for your needs.

39. Virality

👉 *Viral features in applications are one of the most valuable, sought after and difficult parts of building highly successful applications and experiences.*

Virality for products means when a product or its marketing campaign gains widespread attention and adoption, often spreading rapidly among consumers.

As product managers we focus on building virality into the product, not the marketing and advertising side. Our work is often referred to as Product-Led_Growth (PLG).

When a product goes viral, it means that people are enthusiastically sharing information about it, recommending it to others, and generating a buzz through various channels, such as social media and word of mouth both online and offline.

Why people share and tell others about products

The sharing economy, as it's often called, is purely based on human psychology. Understanding human tendencies will equip growth professionals with the reasons why their products gain traction, or not.

Common tendencies include:

Social Validation: people often share products to seek validation from their social circle.

Helpful Recommendations: sharing products is a way to provide helpful recommendations to friends, family, or followers.

Expressing Identity: products can be a reflection of an individual's identity, lifestyle, or values.

FOMO (Fear of Missing Out): people may share to ensure that their friends or followers don't miss out on a great opportunity.

Brand affinity: Individuals often share products to show their affiliation with certain brands.

Social Currency: sharing certain products or experiences can contribute to a person's social currency and elevate their social status or recognition.

Entertainment Value: products that are entertaining, amusing, or have a unique aspect may be shared for the sheer enjoyment of others.

Curation of Personal Brand: sharing products allows individuals to curate and showcase their personal brand.

Incentives and Rewards: a key driver for sharing products is incentivized programs.

Problem-Solving: some people share products that solve a specific problem or address a need.

As you can see a lot of these options are interrelated and play off of each other so even one of these methods can help growth in multiple ways.

Design of viral products

Virality can be created in both single-player and multiplayer products.

- Single player means when the product provides value to a single user without the need for other users to also be there with them.
- Multiplayer means where more than one user is needed to bring the value of the product out.

Multiplayer products, when successful, can have massive network effects and become very difficult for competition to challenge them.

That said, only a few companies have been able to garner multiplayer consumer products so although it's possible it's very difficult.

Single player tools in contrast can take longer to grow but are less dependent on other players to keep engagement with users.

If possible, build single player tools with multiplayer functionality for the best long term growth trajectory.

Multiplayer products enhance usefulness and utility of the product for all users due to the community-like communication and collaboration options and can be an optional feature or the core functionality of a shopping app.

And with the increasingly social, mobile and interconnected nature of all our technology tools the foundation for sharing interesting and valuable apps and services with others is ready, all you need is a compelling and engaging experience.

In the case of ecommerce and shopping, multi-user functionality expands the benefits of shopping by doing it with others, and not alone by yourself.

Many of the topics covered in part Two are a form of product-led-growth tactics, we'll review and add more here.

- Referral programs with discount codes
- Point system in conjunction with loyalty programs
- Sharing features built into the website or app
- Unique and differentiated content and advice
- Enhanced personal profile - consumers like showing their innovative and unique style and will share their personal profile with custom content.
- Followers and comments - providing options to other users to share and comment on another user's profile
- Private groups and communities - access to limited programs available by sharing and bringing your friends

These are some of the options and every product manager is best equipped to experiment and try different viral features based on their in-depth understanding of their customers, products and market.

Example of multiplayer ecommerce - Group shopping

Group shopping refers to a shopping approach where individuals come together as a group to make purchases, often in order to take advantage of discounts, bulk pricing, or other benefits that come with buying in larger quantities.

Group shopping can happen both online and offline, and the gamification factors possible in the online form can result in much better growth.

Group buying offers several benefits for both shoppers and businesses.

Benefits for Shoppers

Discounted Prices: The primary benefit for shoppers is the opportunity to purchase products or services at a discounted rate. Group buying often allows consumers to access significant savings, which can be especially appealing for expensive or luxury items.

Collective Bargaining Power: Group buying gives consumers collective bargaining power. By joining forces with others, shoppers can negotiate better deals, which may not be available to individual buyers.

Sense of Community: Group buying creates a sense of community and shared goals among participants. Shoppers can connect with like-minded individuals, friends, or family members who are interested in the same products or services.

Social Interaction: Group buying apps and platforms often include social features, such as chat, discussion forums, and shared wish lists.

Increased Trust: When shoppers see others participating in a group buying campaign, it can build trust in the deal and the seller.

Access to Exclusive Deals: Group buying often provides access to exclusive deals that are not available through traditional shopping channels.

Benefits for Businesses

Products which can grow using viral effects lead to large outcomes, often leading and owning a category.

In the example of group buying benefits include:

Increased sales: group buying campaigns can lead to a surge in sales volume within a short period. Businesses can reach a wider audience as participants share the deals with their networks.

Accelerated customer acquisition: group buying attracts new customers to the business. Participants may not have been aware of the company or its products before the campaign, potentially leading to long-term customers.

Marketing and brand exposure: group buying campaigns act as marketing events that generate buzz and exposure for the business. This can help raise brand awareness and visibility.

Inventory management: businesses can use group buying to clear excess inventory or promote slow-moving products, helping to manage stock levels effectively.

Cash flow: while businesses may offer products at a lower price during group buying campaigns, they often receive payments upfront, which can help with cash flow.

Data and insights: group buying campaigns provide valuable data about customer preferences and behavior. This information can be used to tailor future marketing efforts and product offerings.

Stickiness and customer loyalty: Businesses that provide a positive group buying experience may foster customer loyalty. Satisfied customers are more likely to return for repeat purchases.

Competitive advantage: offering group buying deals can give a business a competitive edge in the market, setting it apart from competitors and attracting more customers.

40. Wish list

👉 *Wishlists play a crucial role in the growth of ecommerce businesses by enhancing the overall customer experience and driving sales.*

Traditional ecommerce wish lists allow customers to create a list of products they are interested in from the company's catalog, but may not be ready to purchase yet. With the advent of assisted search and shopping techniques and natural language communication capabilities of generative AI the traditional wishlist is going through a transformation to be more useful for consumers.

Wishlists contribute to growth by allowing a higher level of engagement and personalization, providing reminder, notifications and relevant promotions, gifting, social sharing and promoting account creation. All these benefit ecommerce KPIs including AOV and LTV while also helping reduce cart abandonment.

Wish list design

Adding a wishlist to your ecommerce experience requires careful planning and consideration of pros and cons.

The design itself needs to be easy to use for consumers, customizable, mobile optimized, include sharing and potentially group collaborations options as well as reminders and powerful analytics for your use.

If using an external tool API availability is key as well as customer data privacy and tracking.

Examples of wish lists

Amazon: Amazon's wish list functionality allows customers to create multiple lists, add products from anywhere on the site, and share their lists with others.

Sephora: Sephora's wishlist functionality allows customers to create a list of products they are interested in, view product details and ratings, and share their list with others.

Next generation Wish lists

The typical ecommerce and retail wishlist is a way for customers to add an item already on that site to a holding place so it can later be accessed easily in the future.

This requires the shopper to have already done most of the discovery and search work. The discovery and search side of shopping can be time consuming and often frustrating for most people, especially for busy people or people making quick decisions and the typical wish lists do not address this pain point.

The enhanced wish list includes the discovery and recommendations across the Web and local stores so the customer does not have to do all this work by themselves.

There has not been any notable evolution of the wishlist since the early days of online shopping and this opens up potential to expand and upgrade the experience and offer a unique service to your customers.

Measuring success

Measuring the success of wish lists involves tracking several key metrics the main one being the actual usage and number of items added by users. In addition frequency, conversion rate, AOV and LTV contributions are important to track and see how the wishlist is impacting these metrics.

Part Three

Getting into action and continued learning.

How to use the information in this book

Would any of the techniques or capabilities apply to your ecommerce operation? Have you tried some of these and did not get the results you expected?

This is my goal from publishing this book, to give ecommerce product managers and pros a tool chest, or checklist, to go through for their specific products and customer segments.

Not all of these ideas work for every product category or customer and my hope is that having a list to go through you can start evaluating if and which of these you want to start experimenting with.

Commit to action

Information that is not used is wasted, as well as the time spent reading or learning it. It's important to make a dedicated commitment to use what we learn and stay current with new developments.

Many experienced people believe their past experience with a tool or technique in another ecommerce setting gives them sufficient data to assume the same results in a different company and although this may sometimes be correct it is actually often incorrect.

Not only are there differences between products and customer segments, there is also the continuous change in societal, environmental, regulatory and other aspects of the world which have impact.

So if a technique worked well 2 or 3 years ago it does not necessarily mean it will work today even for the same organization let alone different organizations.

This is where the key super powers of product managers and leaders come into play by having a pulse on the market, customers, technology and current growth techniques.

An objective and data-informed mindset is required when deciding which tools to experiment with for your product.

Focus on becoming excellent in designing experiments.

The best experiments are the smallest initiatives which will provide "useful data" for your product or organization.

Useful data is data which is statistically correlated to match from a small sample to a larger audience.

This is something you need to try and learn and see what works for your product, and for each growth technique or tool.

For example Google Optimize requires a minimum number of days and sample units to be able to start predicting the potential success and failure of an experiment to a statistically high probability rate close to 99%.

Ongoing support and training

The sphere of coverage and play for ecommerce and retail product managers is constantly evolving and in multiple dimensions.

Our industry has a non-stop flow of new information, methods, tools, strategies, lessons and insight requiring a non-stor learning system.

In order to stay on top, maintain marketable skills and build and grow profitable products our training can never stop.

Use the information and systems in this book as one pillar of a multi-pillar strategy in your product management and growth journey.

I am happy to offer options I find useful in my experience to my peers and hope to learn from your experiences as we make online shipping better for all of us consumers and our companies.

The next two sections offer additional methods to grow our personal and business lives.

In addition an accompanying website and tool is provided to help with ongoing updates, deep insights and much more.

https://ecomprod.com

Growth scorecard

The following list will help you assess your ecommerce product's growth posture and help you identify opportunity areas.

Since this is a continually evolving topic and list I have created a live version which you as a purchaser of this book have access to https://ecomprod.com/scorecard-growth.

The online version will be updated with new options as well as calculate your score dynamically.

I have added space for making your notes for each item as well as the date you made that assessment so you can come back periodically and see how things have changed.

1. **Account:**
   a. We have a customer account with
      i. Profile
      ii. Order
      iii. Payment
      iv. Custom content
      v. Recommendations
      vi. Cross-sells and upsells
      vii. Packages
      viii. Special deals
      ix. Have analytics
      x. Loyalty program rewards, points, levels, progress to next level, redemption options

Notes: _____

Date: _____

2. Affiliate programs
    a.   We offer an affiliate program
         i.   Directly
        ii.   Through a 3rd party

Notes: _____

Date: _____

3. Advertising and retail media
    a.   We offer advertising to other parties

Notes: _____

Date: _____

4. Analytics
    a.   We have a robust dashboard for all KPIs
    b.   We have automated notifications based on target levels
    c.   We have one or more dashboards
    d.   We have heatmap analysis
    e.   We design and run high level product-level experiments

Notes: _____

Date: _____

5. Bundles and Packages
    a.   We offer bundles
    b.   We offer packages

Notes: _____

Date: _____

6. Chat
    a.   We offer chatbots
    b.   We offer web-chat (human based)

Notes: _____

Date: _____

7. Checkout
    a.   We have guest checkout
    b.   We have 1-click checkout
    c.   We have single-page checkout

Notes: _____

Date: _____

8. Community and customer care
    a.   We have a community
    b.   Our community is active and engaged
    c.   We track attribution to our KPIs from our community

Notes: _____

Date: _____

9. Conversion Rate Optimization
    a.   We run weekly AB tests
    b.   We run concurrent AB tests
    c.   Majority of our AB tests are variant winners

    d. We outsource to a CRO agency

Notes: _____

Date: _____

10. Cross-sells and Up-sells
    a. We use cross-sells
    b. We use up-sells

Notes: _____

Date: _____

11. Direct to consumer
    a. We have a direct-to-consumer channel
    b. We only do D2C

Notes: _____

Date: _____

12. Express sign up
    a. We have express sign ups
    b. We track analytics on our express customer KPIs

Notes: _____

Date: _____

13. Extended reality
    a. We have or have experimented with AR

    b.   We have or have experimented with MR

    c.   We have or have experimented with VR

Notes: _____

Date: _____

14. Fit and size

    a.   We use fit apps on PDP

    b.   We have Size options on PDP

    c.   We have color options on PDP

    d.   We utilize 3D animation

Notes: _____

Date: _____

15. Gamification

    a.   We have gamification features for customers

    b.   We use gamification features for other stakeholders such as partners.

Notes: _____

Date: _____

16. Loyalty programs

    a.   We have a loyalty program

Notes: _____

Date: _____

17. Marketplace
    a.   We have a marketplace
    b.   We sell on marketplaces

Notes: _____

Date: _____

18. Mobile apps
    a.   We have an iOs app
    b.   We have an Android app

Notes: _____

Date: _____

19. Notifications and Reminders
    a.   We use automated email notifications and reminders
    b.   We use automated SMS notifications and reminders
    c.   We use automated Push notifications and reminders

Notes: _____

Date: _____

20. Partnerships and private label
    a.   We have a private label brand
    b.   We have co-branding partnerships
    c.   We have cross-promotion partnerships
    d.   We have a referral program

Notes: _____

Date: _____

21. Payment
    a. We offer 3rd party payments including apple pay
    b. We offer Paypal
    c. We accept all credit cards
    d. We offer split payments
    e. We offer group payment (in gifting use cases)

Notes: _____

Date: _____

22. Personalization
    a. We use a personalization service

Notes: _____

Date: _____

23. Premiumization
    a. We offer premium programs to customers

Notes: _____

Date: _____

24. Pricing strategy
    a. We use dynamic pricing services

Notes: _____

Date: _____

25. Recommendations
      a.   We offer recommendations

Notes: _____

Date: _____

26. Reviews and ratings
      a.   We offer Reviews
      b.   We offer ratings

Notes: _____

Date: _____

27. Returns
      a.   We offer free returns (with or w/o limits)
      b.   We offer BORIS (Buy Online Return In Store)
      c.   We use "Keep it" programs

Notes: _____

Date: _____

28. Rental
      a.   We have a rental program

Notes: _____

Date: _____

29. Resale and re-commerce
   a. We have a resale program
   b. We sell on resale marketplaces / apps

Notes: _____

Date: _____

30. Retention
   a. We have a retention program
   b. We have automated churn-reduction programs

Notes: _____

Date: _____

31. Search
   a. We have text based search
   b. We have facets

Notes: _____

Date: _____

32. Shipping and delivery
   a. We offer free or discounted shipping or delivery
   b. We offer local delivery
   c. We offer BOPIS (Buy-online-pickup-in-store)
   d. We offer Curbside pick up

Notes: _____

Date: _____

33. SMS and messaging commerce
    a. We sell using SMS (including re-orders)
    b. We sell on messaging apps such as WhatsApp

Notes: _____

Date: _____

34. Social commerce
    a. We sell on or experimented with social media selling

Notes: _____

Date: _____

35. Styling and personal shopping
    a. We have a styling program
    b. We work with 3rd party personal shopping services

Notes: _____

Date: _____

36. Stores
    a. We have our own retail stores
    b. We have pop up stores
    c. We have guide shops
    d. We sell through retailers

Notes: _____

Date: _____

37. Subscriptions
    a.   We offer subscriptions

Notes: _____

Date: _____

38. Video
    a.   We have video on PDP
    b.   We use shoppable video
    c.   We offer options for live shopping to customers

Notes: _____

Date: _____

39. Virality
    a.   We utilize viral features across our consumer touch points.

Notes: _____

Date: _____

40. Wishlist
    a.   We have a wish list

Notes: _____

Date: _____

You can add notes and see how you score here or go to the link included above for a web version where you will receive a scope and additional information.

Ecommerce product manager's bookshelf

In closing I'd like to propose a library for ecommerce product managers. This list, in alphabetical order, is selected to develop a well-rounded background for the specific needs and high-expectations from product managers and leaders.

On product management foundations

- **The Art of Product Management**: Lessons from a Silicon Valley Innovator, by Rich Mironov.
- **Business Model Generation**: A Handbook for Visionaries, Game Changers, and Challengers, by Alexander Osterwalder and Yves Pigneur.
- **Business Model You**: A One-Page Method For Reinventing Your Career, by Tim Clark and Alexander Osterwalder.
- **Competing on Analytics**: The New Science of Winning, by Thomas H. Davenport and Jeanne G. Harris.
- **Don't Make Me Think**, Revisited A Common Sense Approach to Web Usability, by Steve Krug.
- **Escaping the Build Trap**: How Effective Product Management Creates Real Value, by Melissa Perri.
- **Hooked**: How to Build Habit-Forming Products, by Nir Eyal.
- **Inspired**: How To Create Products Customers Love, by Marty Cagan. (plus several other great book from the same author)
- **Measure What Matters**: Online Tools for Understanding Customers, Social Media, Engagement, and Key Relationships, by Katie Delahaye Paine.
- **Building Products for the Enterprise**: Product Management in Enterprise Software, by Blair Reeves and Benjamin Gaines.
- **User Experience Revolution**, by Paul Boag.

- **Product Roadmaps Relaunched**: How to Set Direction while Embracing Uncertainty" by C. Todd Lombardo, Bruce McCarthy, Evan Ryan, and Michael Connors.
- **The Product Book**: How to Become a Great Product Manager" by Product School.
- **The Lean Startup**: How Today's Entrepreneurs Use Continuous Innovation to Create Radically Successful Businesses, by Eric Ries.
- **This Is Marketing**: You Can't Be Seen Until You Learn to See, by Seth Godin.
- **User Story Mapping**: Discover the Whole Story, Build the Right Product, by Jeff Patton.

On opportunity identification and market analysis

- **The Amazon Way**: Amazon's 14 Leadership Principles (and series), by John Rossman.
- **The Art of Strategy**: A Game Theorist's Guide to Success in Business and Life, by Avinash K. Dixit and Barry J. Nalebuff.
- **Blitzscaling**: The Lightning-Fast Path to Building Massively Valuable Companies, by Reid Hoffman and Chris Yeh.
- **Blue Ocean Strategy**: How to Create Uncontested Market Space and Make the Competition Irrelevant, by W. Chan Kim and Renée Mauborgne.
- **Competing Against Luck**: The Story of Innovation and Customer Choice, by Clayton M. Christensen.
- **Competitive Strategy**: Techniques for Analyzing Industries and Competitors, by Michael E. Porter.
- **Crossing the Chasm**: Marketing and Selling Disruptive Products to Mainstream Customers, by Geoffrey A. Moore.

- **The Everything Store**: Jeff Bezos and the Age of Amazon, by Brad Stone.
- **The Innovator's Dilemma**: When New Technologies Cause Great Firms to Fail, by Clayton M. Christensen.
- **Thinking, Fast and Slow**, by Daniel Kahneman.
- **Zero to One**: Notes on Startups, or How to Build the Future, by Peter Thiel.

On ecommerce principles

- **E-Commerce Blueprint**: The Step-by-Step Guide to Online Store Success, by Rob Mabry.
- **E-Commerce Book**: Building the E-Empire, by Alex Jeffrey.
- **E-Commerce Book**: 10 Steps to Setting Up an Online Store for Small Business, by Qasim Rasi.
- **E-commerce Evolved**: Essential To Build, Grow & Scale a Successful E-commerce Business, by Tanner Larsson.
- **E-Commerce for Dummies**, by Don Jones and Mark D. Scott.
- **E-Commerce Get It Right!**: Essential Step-by-Step Guide for Selling & Marketing Products Online, by Ian Daniel.
- **Ecom Hell**: How to Make Money in Ecommerce Without Getting Burned, by Shirley Tan.
- **E-Commerce Operations and Management**, by David Walters and Dave Walters.
- **E-Commerce Website Design and Development**: A Practical Guide, by Paul Bradish.
- **E-Commerce Marketing**: How to Get Traffic That BUYS to Your Website, by Richard Webster.
- **E-Commerce Marketing Strategy**: A Definitive Guide to Sustainable and Scalable Growth, by Joris Bryon.

- **Invisible Selling Machine**, by Ryan Deiss.
- **The Long Tail**: Why the Future of Business is Selling Less of More, by Chris Anderson.

On experimentation and analytics

- **Ecommerce Analytics**: Analyze and Improve the Impact of Your Digital Strategy, by Judah Phillips.
- **Experimentation Works**: The Surprising Power of Business Experiments, by Stefan H. Thomke - Stefan Thomke.
- **Experimentation Matters**: Unlocking the Potential of New Technologies for Innovation, by Stefan H. Thomke.
- **Experimentation in Software Engineering**: by Claes Wohlin and Per Runeson.
- **Experiment!**: Website conversion rate optimization with A/B and multivariate testing, by Colin McFarland.
- **The Growth Marketer's Playbook**: A Strategic Guide to Growing a Business in Today's Digital World, by Jim Huffman.
- **The Lean Product and Lean Analytics Collection**, by Ben Yoskovitz and Alistair Croll.
- **Optimal Product Process**: Using the Data-Driven Product Manager Approach, by Henry Liu.
- **Testing Business Ideas**: A Field Guide for Rapid Experimentation, by David J. Bland and Alexander Osterwalder.
- **Thinking, Testing, Doing**: A Framework for Experimentation in Business, by Morgan Brown and Sean Ellis.
- **Web Analytics 2.0**: The Art of Online Accountability and Science of Customer Centricity, by Avinash Kaushik.

On experiment design

- **A/B Testing**: The Most Powerful Way to Turn Clicks Into Customers, by Dan Siroker and Pete Koomen.
- **The Conversion Code**: Capture Internet Leads, Create Quality Appointments, Close More Sales, by Chris Smith.
- **Design and Analysis of Experiments**, by Douglas C. Montgomery.
- **Designing Experiments and Analyzing Data**: A Model Comparison Perspective, by Scott E. Maxwell, Harold D. Delaney, and Ken Kelley.
- **E-Commerce Website Optimization**: Why 95% of Your Website Visitors Don't Buy, and What You Can Do About It, by Dan Croxen-John and Johann van Tonder.
- **Experiment!**: Website Conversion Rate Optimization with A/B and Split Testing, by Colin McFarland.
- **Practical Experiment Design for Engineers and Scientists**, by Stephen R. Schmidt.
- **Split Testing Mastery**: Unlocking the True Potential of Split Testing, by Adrian Landsberg.
- **Statistical Models**: Theory and Practice, by David A. Freedman and Robert Pisani.
- **Testing Statistical Hypotheses**, by Erich L. Lehmann and Joseph P. Romano.
- **Trustworthy Online Controlled Experiments**: A Practical Guide to A/B Testing, by Ron Kohavi, Diane Tang, and Ya Xu.

On growth

- **The Growth Marketer's Playbook**: A Strategic Guide to Growing a Business in Today's Digital World, by Jim Huffman.
- **Hacking Growth**: How Today's Fastest-Growing Companies Drive Breakout Success, by Sean Ellis and Morgan Brown.
- **The Innovator's Solution**: Creating and Sustaining Successful Growth, by Clayton M. Christensen and Michael E. Raynor.
- **The Lean Growth Machine**: How Innovative Startups Use Lean Methodologies to Grow, by Trevor Owens and Obie Fernandez.
- **Measure What Matters**: Online Tools for Understanding Customers, Social Media, Engagement, and Key Relationships, by Katie Delahaye Paine.
- **Traction**: How Any Startup Can Achieve Explosive Customer Growth, by Gabriel Weinberg and Justin Mares.
- **Scaling Up**: How a Few Companies Make It...and Why the Rest Don't, by Verne Harnish.
- **The Ultimate Guide to E-Commerce Growth**: How to Grow by 30% or More in 90 Days Using a 5-Step Repeatable Process, by Daniel Tejada.

On agile development

- **Agile Estimating and Planning**, by Mike Cohn.
- **Agile Retrospectives**: Making Good Teams Great, by Esther Derby and Diana Larsen.
- **Agile Testing**: A Practical Guide for Testers and Agile Teams, by Lisa Crispin and Janet Gregory.
- **Continuous Delivery**: Reliable Software Releases through Build, Test, and Deployment Automation, by Jez Humble and David Farley.

- **Essential Scrum**: A Practical Guide to the Most Popular Agile Process, by Kenneth S. Rubin.
- **Kanban**: Successful Evolutionary Change for Your Technology Business, by David J. Anderson.
- **Lean-Agile Software Development**: Achieving Enterprise Agility, by Alan Shalloway, Guy Beaver, and James R. Trott.
- **Scrum**: The Art of Doing Twice the Work in Half the Time, by Jeff Sutherland.
- **Sprint:** How to Solve Big Problems and Test New Ideas in Just Five Days, by Jake Knapp.
- **User Stories Applied**: For Agile Software Development, by Mike Cohn.

On team building and collaboration

- **Building a StoryBrand**: Clarify Your Message So Customers Will Listen, by Donald Miller.
- **Collaborative Intelligence**: Thinking with People Who Think Differently, by Dawna Markova and Angie McArthur.
- **Crucial Conversations**: Tools for Talking When Stakes Are High, by Kerry Patterson, Joseph Grenny, Ron McMillan, and Al Switzler.
- **The Culture Code**: The Secrets of Highly Successful Groups, by Daniel Coyle.
- **Drive**: The Surprising Truth About What Motivates Us, by Daniel H. Pink.
- **The Five Dysfunctions of a Team**: A Leadership Fable, by Patrick Lencioni.

- **The Five-Stage Team Development Model**: How to Transform Purpose-Driven Teams to Powerhouse Organizations, by Shawn Kent Hayashi.
- **Radical Candor**: Be a Kick-Ass Boss Without Losing Your Humanity, by Kim Scott.
- **Team Geek**: A Software Developer's Guide to Working Well with Others, by Ben Collins-Sussman, Jenny Greene, and Matthew McCullough.
- **Team of Teams**: New Rules of Engagement for a Complex World, by General Stanley McChrystal.

On handling failure

- **Antifragile**: Things that Gain from Disorder, by Nassim Nicholas Taleb.
- **Black Box Thinking**: Why Most People Never Learn from Their Mistakes—But Some Do, by Matthew Syed.
- **Fail, Fail Again, Fail Better**: Wise Advice for Leaning into the Unknown, by Pema Chödrön.
- **Daring Greatly**: How the Courage to Be Vulnerable Transforms the Way We Live, Love, Parent, and Lead, by Brené Brown.
- **Failing Forward**: Turning Mistakes into Stepping Stones for Success, by John C. Maxwell.
- **Mindset**: The New Psychology of Success, by Carol S. Dweck.
- **The Obstacle is the Way**: The Timeless Art of Turning Trials into Triumph, by Ryan Holiday.
- **Resilience**: Hard-Won Wisdom for Living a Better Life, by Eric Greitens.
- **The Gifts of Imperfection**: Let Go of Who You Think You're Supposed to Be and Embrace Who You Are, by Brené Brown.

- **You Are a Badass**: How to Stop Doubting Your Greatness and Start Living an Awesome Life, by Jen Sincero.

On how to stay relevant

- **Deep Work**: Rules for Focused Success in a Distracted World, by Cal Newport.
- **The Fourth Industrial Revolution,** by Klaus Schwab.
- **Grit**: The Power of Passion and Perseverance, by Angela Duckworth.
- **Learning How to Learn**: How to Succeed in School Without Spending All Your Time Studying; A Guide for Kids and Teens, by Barbara Oakley and Terrence Sejnowski.
- **Never Stop Learning**: Stay Relevant, Reinvent Yourself, and Thrive, by Bradley R. Staats.
- **Range**: Why Generalists Triumph in a Specialized World, by David Epstein.
- **The Start-Up of You**: Adapt to the Future, Invest in Yourself, and Transform Your Career, by Reid Hoffman and Ben Casnocha.
- **Stealing Fire**: How Silicon Valley, the Navy SEALs, and Maverick Scientists Are Revolutionizing the Way We Live and Work, by Steven Kotler and Jamie Wheal.

On handling change

- **The Change Book**: How Things Happen, by Mikael Krogerus and Roman Tschäppeler.

- **Drive**: The Surprising Truth About What Motivates Us, by Daniel H. Pink.
- **The Heart of Change**: Real-Life Stories of How People Change Their Organizations, by John P. Kotter and Dan S. Cohen.
- **Our Iceberg Is Melting**: Changing and Succeeding Under Any Conditions, by John Kotter and Holger Rathgeber.
- **Leading Change**, by John P. Kotter.
- **Managing Transitions**: Making the Most of Change, by William Bridges.
- **The Power of Habit**: Why We Do What We Do in Life and Business, by Charles Duhigg.
- **Switch**: How to Change Things When Change Is Hard, by Chip Heath and Dan Heath.
- **Switchers**: How Smart Professionals Change Careers and Seize Success, by Dr. Dawn Graham.
- **Who Moved My Cheese?**, by Dr. Spencer Johnson.

A living list can be found on https://ecomprod.com/bookshelf. I have surely missed some great books and would love recommendations.

. end

Publisher: BooDaa Publishing, a unit of InfiniVentures Labs.

ecomprod.com is a product of InfiniVentures Labs.

www.ingramcontent.com/pod-product-compliance
Lightning Source LLC
Chambersburg PA
CBHW050436290526
45786CB00006B/2053